I0029775

ROUND-UP
A GATHERING OF EQUINE WRITINGS

ROUND-UP
A GATHERING OF EQUINE WRITINGS

Tom Moates

SPINNING SEVENS
PRESS

Copyright © 2011 by Tom Moates

ALL RIGHTS RESERVED. No part of this book may be
reproduced or transmitted in any form by any means, electronic
or mechanical, including photocopying and recording, or by any
information storage and retrieval system, except as may be expressly
permitted in writing from the publisher. Requests for permission
should be addressed to Spinning Sevens Press, Attn: Rights and
Permissions, P. O. Box 440, Floyd, Virginia, 24091.

978-0-9845850-2-1

Created June 2011
Designed by Chris Legg

Cover photo by Carol Moates

TABLE OF CONTENTS

FOREWORD

The realm of journalism one might term "the equestrian media" is blessed with a sizable population of gifted writers, those who approach their work with genuine respect for their craft and solid foundations in the horse culture. Such correspondents transport readers to the arenas of the world's most gifted horsemen and artfully set scenes in which complex, esoteric techniques are boiled to their essence, then reinterpreted for the masses in reader-friendly fashion.

Within this group of writers, though, only a painfully small minority write from places of personal inspiration, allowing their own questions about horsemanship to guide the creative process. It's little wonder, as such intimate approaches carry considerable risks. For one, editors are hesitant to venture outside the proverbial box and forsake reliable formulas for previously untested strategies, no matter how well suited those strategies might seem for the subjects at hand. Ironically, writers who dare to approach their work with such originality risk crippling their careers as their phone messages and e-mails go unreturned and assignments are handed to contributors who take safer, if less innovative, routes. And, writers who work from such places of honesty leave themselves vulnerable, potentially revealing to readers the kinds of weaknesses that most folks prefer to keep deeply hidden.

Horsemanship, though, is a field defined by seemingly endless nuance, an indefinable and evolving cloud of questions and half-answers that its master practitioners describe as "feel." It is an art, not a science. With horses, outcomes are not predictable; rules are never hard and fast; and archetypes are elusive. Given such a shifting landscape, one can argue that this avocation's most meaningful lessons are not conveyed by scribes working safely within the confines of established formats; rather, its most useful insights are likely to come from writers who can muster the strength to draw upon their own experiences and honestly share both their victories and setbacks as they draft material meant to both instruct and inspire.

Tom Moates is one such writer. In telling the story of his own evolution as a horseman and his ongoing work in forging meaningful connections with horses, Tom has offered his readers a refreshing message, a signal of clarity amidst the white noise of the horse world's marketing-driven media and its promises of easy solutions to horse-handling challenges. The lesson he offers: horsemanship is an endless journey, one in which each answer brings with it new questions, and while such an odyssey is unlikely to reveal the unwavering edicts so many of us think we desire, it can nonetheless offer those armed with adequate patience a chance to discover an ever-expanding set of tools for understanding one of nature's most rewarding, yet most perplexing, partnerships.

In his book *Zen and the Art of Motorcycle Maintenance,* author Robert Pirsig blends a compelling narrative about a cross-country motorcycle trip with a detailed treatise on the definition of *quality* and the tenets of a philosophy in which aesthetics and functionality must necessarily coexist. *Zen . . .* is an oft-cited benchmark for any book in which an author attempts to find answers to potentially overwhelming questions. The book that propelled Tom to the forefront of equestrian journalism, *Discovering Natural Horsemanship,* is worthy of the comparison, as it tells an irresistible story of its author's discovery of "the Better Way with horses," while confirming for readers that they are not alone in their search for meaningful answers to their own potentially overwhelming questions about horse-handling.

Tom's follow-up books, *A Horse's Thought* and *Between the Reins,* are equally powerful, chronicling his efforts to grow as a horseman under the tutelage of his mentor, clinician Harry Whitney. Taken as a trilogy, the three volumes offer a rare look at a horseman's progression over time from neophyte to veteran rider, one for whom each new piece of wisdom holds the promise of yet another previously undiscovered branch of study. Tom shares his pursuit of answers with a brand of journalism fueled by an intellectual curiosity his peers in the equestrian media would be wise to emulate, providing in the end a wisdom forged by observations, impressions and firsthand experiences.

Horsemanship is, for each of us, a personal journey. And no one tells the story of his journey through the world of horses better than Tom Moates.

A.J. Mangum
Pueblo, Colorado
May 2011

ACKNOWLEDGEMENTS

Without editorial interest in my work, the bulk of the articles and essays in this compilation would not have been written, let alone published. Many thanks to all the magazine editors who have accepted my queries over the years. The assignments allowed me to stay busy with one of my greatest passions—writing about horses.

A very special thanks goes to A. J. Mangum, not only for his role as the former editor of *Western Horseman* magazine who coordinated with me on several of the articles re-printed here, but also for contributing the foreword to this book. I'm very excited he agreed to write it even though he is busy with many new projects these days, like the ongoing video documentary series he created: The Frontier Project (www.thefrontierproject.com).

Thanks to Christine Barakat, a Senior Editor at *Equus* magazine who has been a great support for as long as I've been writing about horses. Also, thanks to Emily Kitching, owner and editor of *Eclectic-Horseman* magazine (www.eclectic-horseman.com) who has been of immeasurable help keeping both my magazine and book writing moving forward—she and her husband, Steve Bell, also design and host my website (www.TomMoates.com), for which I am enormously grateful. The whole staff at the American Quarter Horse Association (www.AQHA.com) is fantastic and I always greatly enjoy the writing I am able to do for both *America's Horse* magazine and *The American Quarter Horse Journal*; several of those stories are included in this volume, so thanks especially to Jim Bret Campbell, Holly Clanahan, Christine Hamilton, Becky Newell, and Larri Jo Starkey for all they've done for this writer over the years. Thanks to Geoff Young, editor and owner of *Horse Connection Magazine* (www. horseconnection.com), for being open to quite a range of story subjects. A regional magazine in Virginia and Maryland, *Horse Talk* (www.horsetalkmagazine.com), ran a couple of the stories from this book and I'd like to thank the editor and owner, Lois Baird, for her interest in my work. Sandy Hannan, editor, and Carol Willcocks, assistant editor, of *Hoofbeats* magazine (www.hoofbeats.com.au) in Australia have re-printed some of the articles compiled here, and I greatly appreciate their support and help editing my material for the Aussie audience.

The photographs used in this book had to be arranged separately from any original magazine publication layouts. I've been extremely fortunate to have lined up such an amazing array of pictures to illustrate this book and I am indebted and tremendously grateful to all of those who were so willing to take the time to provide the images needed for these stories in book form. The credits for them, and any contact information when applicable, are provided with each photo throughout the book. I'd also like to name names here and thank all the photographers and/or image owners individually and alphabetically: Susan Bibb, Tony Bynum, John Egenes, Jerry Ellerman, Dr. Kim Gemeinhardt, David Hart, Jim Jennings, Emily Kitching, Ann Lunak, Carol Moates, Ken Moates, Bob Moorhouse, Walter Nelson, Sally O'Connor (and Walter M. Ball on the same photo), Sled Reynolds, Mary Rudloff, and Allen Russell.

Chris Legg is the virtuoso graphic design artist who once again has done an inspired job creating a cover and book lay out with just the right feel and balance. The hours he devoted to this book, as with the latest version of *A Horse's Thought* and my recent book, *Between the Reins,* is appreciated beyond words.

Finally, I'd like to express immeasurable gratitude to Kelly Robinson of Montana, my editor on this book. Her long hours, (Masters degree in English!), tenacity, and personal momentum for the project are truly what moved it along and certainly the very reason so many wrinkles were smoothed out. Since we worked from my original drafts for the articles provided as chapters in this book, her job was difficult indeed, and the improvements and corrections she suggested are the reason for the wonderful high quality you'll find in these pages.

INTRODUCTION

Horses fascinate me. Each day I set out to learn more about them. I tumble along these days, pulled by some strange gravity to explore all kinds of different aspects of the equine world. And I love to share what I discover. Apparently that is the recipe for a successful equestrian journalist and author, and I'm blessed to work in this field.

Ever since being smitten by horses about a decade ago, my writing career snowballed. I've contributed articles to many national and regional horse magazines in the United States, as well as seeing my work published in England and Australia. Magazine articles, however, are doomed to a very short shelf life.

Horse books, however, seem to hold up better to the passing of time. They enter the equine literature and remain ground tied there. *A Horse's Thought* and *Between the Reins,* the two memoirs chronicling my work with horsemanship clinician Harry Whitney (www.harrywhitney.com) for example, do not disappear. They are right there on the shelves in libraries and homes and remain "in print," unlike their periodical cousins.

This book compiles some wonderful and timeless horse-based articles and essays between two covers and solves the shelf-life dilemma. Many of the horses, people, and subjects I've had the good fortune to write about over the years are amazing, and I'm delighted to breathe new life into their stories with this volume. *Round-Up: A Gathering of Equine Writings*, does just that . . . it rounds-up quite a few strays and provides the opportunity to showcase some of my favorites from over the years. I've dusted them off and in many cases provided original material previously edited out due to space constraints. I hope this book allows readers for many years to come to enjoy some notable horse-based stories that otherwise had faded from view.

Tom Moates
May 2011

CHAPTER 1

The O'Connors stop along the trail to let the horses drink—8 and 10 hour
days were typical for them on the journey.
(Walter M. Ball)

A CROSS COUNTRY RIDE LIKE NO OTHER

---

*David O'Connor is internationally renowned for his many accomplishments
in three-day eventing, including winning three Olympic medals. In 2009, he was
inducted into the USEA Eventing Hall of Fame. Somewhere along the line as I
worked on various equestrian articles, I came across an obscure mention of a cross
country ride (that is an equestrian odyssey across the Unites States) O'Connor took*

as a boy. Immediately my interest spiked and I pursued the story.

 The resulting feature article ran in the April 2007 issue of Equus magazine. It marked several firsts for me and thus seems appropriate to begin this compilation. This chapter is my original draft of the story. It was the first time I wrote about a long distance horseback journey—a subject I revisited as a writer many times over the next several years. The article became the first of a string of features I wrote for Equus on David and his wife, Karen O'Connor, and their successful eventing endeavors. It also was the first award winning magazine work for me, taking third place for the year from American Horse Publications for feature articles in magazines with a circulation of over 20,000.

 The name David O'Connor used in conjunction with the term cross-country likely conjures up images of a frothy horse and helmeted rider jumping oxers and splashing through small ponds. The correlation fits since O'Connor spent nearly a decade as a top ranked three-day eventer: his rap sheet includes multiple Olympic medals—among them the individual gold in the 2000 Sydney games—and now he has retired from competition to the office of president of the United States Equestrian Federation.

 At age 11, however, O'Connor already was horseback and getting media attention for riding cross-country: not around a course, but literally across the country from coast to coast. The young boy took a trip of nearly 3000 miles horseback with his mother, Sally (a well known equestrian in her own right with nine books to her credit on horses), and older brother, Brian, riding from Maryland to Oregon.

 When he was ten years old, O'Connor admits his parents weren't getting along very well. The family of four was splintering and ultimately his parents would divorce. Their home at the time was Gaithersburg, Maryland, and had been since his early childhood.

 Sally grew up in England. She says she never intended to make the United States her home. It was merely a stop on her way to Australia, but she married Jay, a Navy man, and settled down and had a family. She worked at the Potomac Horse Center during this time, and both O'Connor and his brother, two and a half years his senior, began their acquaintances with horses early in life.

"I always wanted to do something like that," Sally says of crossing the continent horseback. The seed had been sown in her earlier as she had read books like Aimé Tschiffely's *A Tale of Two Horses* which recounted the author's 10,000 mile journey horseback from Buenos Aires to Washington, D.C. written from the horses' perspectives.

During this time Sally got the idea for the trip. Spurred on, according to O'Connor, by a dinner conversation between her and Brian about another book, *Kon-Tiki*, and the odyssey it conveys about a character crossing the ocean on a raft, his mother started thinking about riding all the way across the continent with her boys. None of them had been out west before, and exploring that country from horseback seemed straight out of a western movie and added to the allure of the endeavor. Once the seed for the idea sprouted, it took firm root with her and quickly grew in the fertile situation of the time.

O'Connor's mother had several conversations about planning the trip with friends, many of whom were completely flabbergasted with disbelief. O'Connor and Sally both say that this only redoubled her determination back then to take the trip with her young boys. She set about working out the details.

"It was probably the only time we could do it," she realizes reflecting on the trip's timing. "David and Brian were 11 and 13 . . . before, and David would have been too young, and later, Brian would have been too old. I really had no idea if you could do it."

"We knew she was serious," O'Connor says about the plans. Then he adds, "As an 11 year old, you don't know the scope of what it will do to go on such a trip. It's a great adventure when you're 11."

The original plan was to head for California. After much deliberation and careful scrutiny of maps of the terrain, that idea was abandoned as less practical than following the Oregon Trail, which runs along rivers most of the way and avoids passing through the desert. There were a handful of family friends from the horse world peppered along their planned route in West Virginia, Indiana, Illinois, and Nebraska. Plans were made to stay with them for respites from the road.

The Journey Begins

They lined up horses for the journey. Sally was eventing at the intermediate level with her mount, Gung Ho, and decided to ride the bay Canadian Thoroughbred on the trip. The ponies the boys had weren't well suited for the task, so she asked around to find them horses to use.

"You don't need anything fancy," she advises would-be long distance riders, "just something solid."

There was nothing fancy about the horses borrowed for the two youngsters, but they were good, sound geldings. B.G., as if testimony to the preceding statements, stood for "Black Gelding," and was a neighbor's retired Pony Club horse that Brian would ride. He was 15 years old, which caused some concern for taking him on such a long journey. A vet checked him over with that question in mind before they decided to depart with him. Sally says that after the exam, "The vet replied, 'He's onery enough he just might make it' . . . and he was right!" In fact, B.G. would be the only horse to make it the entire distance.

The horse chosen for O'Connor was a Quarter Horse mix named Ralph, and he was at the other end of the spectrum: four years old and fairly green. They borrowed him from Ray Little, a friend of Sally's that sold horses and trailers in Maryland. Ralph had one troublesome idiosyncrasy for this kind of journey—he didn't like getting his feet wet. This caused a bit of trouble, according to Sally, when they needed to cross any standing water. To make this even more challenging at the start, "It rained the whole first month just awful!" she remembers.

"My mother was definitely the leader," O'Connor says. "I was pretty much a passenger."

With his mother in the lead, figuratively and literally, it was fitting that the trip began on Mother's Day, May 13, 1973. The crew departed from White's Ferry, Maryland, heading west along the tow path of the old C & O Canal. They traveled light, carrying only an extra set of clothing, sleeping bags, rain ponchos of a type that could double as tents, food, a set of farrier's tools, and a big nylon sack of oats that O'Connor got to carry across his lap since he was the lightest rider. The gear was a bit cumbersome situated around their English saddles. O'Connor recalls times when both he and Ralph had abrasions from clothing and tack rubbing against them, mile after mile.

They wore jeans, hiking boots (since they would be on foot quite a bit at times) and chaps. The chaps were made for the O'Connors by a local saddlery in Maryland, and were constructed from tuff leather and of a western type called shotgun chaps that cover the whole leg tightly from hip to foot. The same shop also built them custom saddle bags which were much bigger than normal and quite deep to provide adequate room for their provisions.

"Our pace was fast," O'Connor explains. "[We rode] eight to ten hours a day. We traveled 30 to 35 miles a day."

Some days, however, they never made 20 miles, and on their best day they covered an impressive 48 miles. It was a tiring pace. One time in West Virginia O'Connor even fell asleep in the saddle, awakening when he hit the ground. The family got into a rhythm of riding for eight days, and then taking two or three off to give the horses (and humans) some down-time to recuperate.

The horses ate their oats from nose bags at stops. They chose oats, according to Sally, since they can be gotten anywhere along the way. When pasture was available, the horses were allowed to graze, and people frequently provided them with hay at stops.

The very first night, however, the O'Connors learned a valuable lesson about pasturing their mounts; they stayed in Maryland at a place that provided them an eight acre pasture for the horses—it took three hours the next morning to catch them.

Across the course of the trip, they over-nighted in nearly every conceivable situation: sleeping on picnic tables at rest areas was common, staying in barns, sleeping on the side of the road, and sometimes even getting invited to stay in a house with the comforts of a real bed.

Not long into the journey, the O'Connor's confronted their first distressing situation—a West Virginia river gorge. The canal path they followed crossed a river on a narrow stone aqueduct. The alternative to crossing the chasm at that point was to back-track three days and cross the river on a highway bridge. All three dismounted and cautiously walked the horses across the flat bridge, scarcely six feet wide. They made it to the other side without incident, but it was this eye opening experience that fixed in their minds the true gravity of the adventure that lay before them.

"We had some dreadful storms," Sally remembers. "In Illinois there was one, the sky was sort of green, kind of like the beginning of *The Wizard of Oz*. The telephone wires were singing. When we got to the Mississippi, it was flooded. I wanted to avoid cities, but we had to cross through Indianapolis because the ferry where we planned to cross was out."

The trip, even with its challenges, progressed mostly according to plan. They covered an acceptable average daily mileage. Most days they rode until the late afternoon when they began knocking on random farmhouse doors to find a place to stay for the night. O'Connor says he especially enjoyed the opportunity to play with other kids when they were around at these stops. During the entire three month journey, the family was only turned away three times when showing up out-of-the-blue at a door and asking to stay overnight. Perhaps it was the novelty of the situation, or maybe the fact that it was a mother traveling with two children, and in some cases the media coverage alerted local people to their presence which helped as well, but O'Connor recalls many people they stayed with became quite protective of them. Often they would try to help out with meals, advice about the road ahead, and sometimes lining up other places where the family might stay in the future.

After riding through Ohio (where one of the highlights was pulling into a drive-in restaurant in Chillicothe among cars, ordering a meal, and getting to see the surprise of the waitress when she came out with their order), Indiana, Illinois, and Iowa, they picked up the Oregon Trail in Nebraska.

"We were on secondary roads 99% of the time," O'Connor

explains. The roads follow the trail closely, so it was not an excursion through the wilderness as in former times. The mileage, however, still remains they same, as do some of the old landmarks. Some stand out in O'Connor's mind as interesting places where they stayed. One such place is Fort Kearny (the actual fort), and Fort Kearney (the nearby city—notice the extra "e") in Nebraska. War Department records from 1849 show that in the 18 months prior to that date, 30,000 people passed through the area headed west, no doubt depending on as many horses, and feeling the wear and tear of the road much like this modern day family and their mounts. In particular, O'Connor remembers the fort because it was also a home station for the Pony Express and they took a little time there to be tourists.

"David really enjoyed the history," Sally recalls, "and Brian enjoyed the people. In Scottsbluff, Nebraska we actually rode down the ruts from the wagon train."

Along the trail in Nebraska, the most dangerous moment of the entire journey occurred, reminiscent of that first brush with danger in West Virginia.

"It's a moment that we all still talk about," O'Connor says. "Some people had driven up and asked if we would stay with them. It was further than we thought [to their place]."

As a result, darkness was closing in on the three riders and their horses when they saw the exit they needed. They turned off the highway onto the road, which lead straight across a narrow bridge. This bridge was two lanes wide and spanned a ravine that dropped 400 feet to the bottom. Riding the horses across it was an uneasy endeavor on its own. All was going well and the were in the center of the span, when suddenly a tractor trailer appeared, heading their way, head-on, rolling at least 70 miles per hour.

"It was a long bridge," O'Connor recalls, and he happened to be out in front of the pack this time for a change. "He was driving right down the middle of the road."

In a matter of seconds, the truck was right on the trail riders. O'Connor figures the driver never saw them until he was right on top of them. He recalls being so close to the speeding rig that the rivets from the trailer were clearly visible when it blew by.

"Our horses never missed a beat," he says, still amazed, and grateful, about the fact to this day.

As the trip continued to unfold, other challenges presented themselves. The pace was taxing to the horses.

"The hardest part about it was to get enough food into them," O'Connor says. "They were getting quite skinny." The oats he and Ralph toted for the horses, along with finding hay and opportunities to graze along the way kept the horses in good health, but he remembers them becoming very lean and fit in a wiry way as the trip progressed.

While still in Nebraska, Ralph's abrasion on a wither from the oat sack became infected, despite the attempt, hundreds of miles earlier, of placing a foam pad between his hide and the bag to fix the unremitting trouble. The resulting fistulous wither meant Ralph would have to quit the trip. One of their regular random stops at that point happened to be at an Arabian breeding farm with around 600 horses. The owner, Ellis Ruby, offered to let them leave Ralph there to convalesce and let O'Connor swap him for an Arabian/ Thoroughbred cross of his. The horse turned out being very well suited for the task of taking on the Oregon Trail (O'Connor eventually named him Jim Bridger in honor of his frontiersman-like skills), but at first the young boy cried buckets of tears for the loss of his long time companion, Ralph.

Sally also would not make it all the way to the west coast with her mount. Gung Ho had reared when being lead into a barn and hit his back on a low doorway back in Illinois. The injury had been apparent, and she had attempted to bulk the padding under the saddle to help alleviate the discomfort on the horse and they had managed to continue fairly well. A few weeks later in Wyoming, however, it was obvious the horse could not continue on the trip. Local people became aware of the family's plight and worked out a young, not-so-broke mare for her to use to continue the journey with her sons. Windy Winter was her name, a chestnut Quarter Horse/ Tennessee Walking Horse mix. Her nickname was "Muley," which suited her personality perfectly, Sally recalls.

This leg of the trip brought another interesting turn of events as well—getting lost in the Rocky Mountains.

"We were in Wyoming," O'Connor recalls, "and we went from Dubious, and cut across and straightened the curve [of a large loop in the road]. The people we were staying with said it was totally do-able."

The family got turned around in the mountainous terrain of that short cut and became lost. As the day faded into night, they never found their way to a road, but did come across a flock of grazing sheep. A shepherd tended them and had a wagon outfitted for camping where he lived for the season while he cared for the animals. They were able to stay the night at his camp, and he directed them on their way in the morning.

"In Jackson Hole, Wyoming, the same thing happened," O'Connor admits of another attempt to cut off some highway miles by riding the horses straight across the country.

The family made it all the way to Oregon as planned and hoped. The boys had cut three weeks off the last school year to get started on the trip, so they ended the trip a few weeks short of reaching the Pacific Ocean so they would not be late for the beginning of the new school year in September back in Maryland. But they were not let down. They had succeeded at their goal and crossed the continent.

When asked if she would recommend such a trip to others these days, she says, "Yes . . . but be warned it is not nearly as glamorous as it seems! It sounds terribly exciting, but it's not. It's terribly dull. It was the people that made it worthwhile."

Sally says the trip offered no foreshadowing that made her think O'Connor might make horses part of his life and livelihood. What the trip did do for the young boy, according to his mother, is, "It gave him the ability to stick with things." A quality no doubt essential to a successful career in eventing.

The lasting effects of the odyssey on O'Connor, he admits, are many. Two, however, stand out in particular to him. When asked about this, he always points first to, "All the different levels of people we met."

O'Connor says he experienced the generosity of such a cross-section of the population, that it profoundly influenced his understanding of people and dissolved barriers that might otherwise have existed within him. To this day, because of those experiences, he is better equipped to understand folks from all walks of life. This has greatly enhanced his ability to take on the roles he has played in his eventing career, because that world brings him constantly into contact with all different kinds of people.

"I realized how close I am with animals," O'Connor says of the other main point from the trip. "It was a strength with me right from the beginning."

His partner was his horse, he says. He reminisces that at the time there were no walkmans, cell phones, portable video games, or portable computers. Without entertainment for 3000 miles, he says, it was just, "Me and Ralph."

CHAPTER 2

Jerome and Tiffany Davis with a group of young cowboys and cowgirls attending their camp. *(David Hart [www.hartphotos.us])*

GIVING BACK

Jerome and Tiffany Davis are amazing, giving tremendous energy to help young people every chance they get. Some very accomplished young bull riders have been coached to success in recent years by Jerome. The couple also raise some of the top bucking bulls in the country today. Tiffany organizes He Paid Your Fees, a Christian junior rodeo put on annually in October at the Davis Ranch Arena in Archdale, North Carolina, which has become one of the largest junior rodeos east of the Mississippi. In 2006, this article ran in the September/ October issue of America's Horse *(www.AQHA.com) highlighting some of the time they devote to teaching youngsters about horses and rodeo. More on the Davises and the many events they have on their busy schedule are listed at www. jeromedavis.com.*

———————————————————

"Hey, cattle! Hey, cattle!" the half dozen cowhands call. "Hey, cattle!"

Five young world-class bucking bulls, each with a full set of horns, move easily along the fence toward a pen at one end of the dusty outdoor arena, as the riders move their mounts along, slowly encouraging the herd forward. The North Carolina sun blazes down on the scene, but the riders squint out from under the shade of their hats to scrutinize the herd's movement. As the crew approaches the open gate, the wing man moves along the side of the herd to turn it into the holding pen, but he gets a little close and crowds them. The herd stalls, then starts to back up and turn.

"When you're a wing man, you've got to stay a little bit further to the side," a voice rings out clearly over the others, still trying to command the cattle to go back toward the gate. It's Tiffany Davis on foot close by, overseeing the cattle drive. "If you get a little too close, they'll turn around on you," she coaches the cowboy.

The wing man reins his horse to the side then encourages him to move by gently bouncing his legs against the horse's sides. The horse gets the idea, even if the rider's boots are a good 10 inches above the stirrups. The cowboys and cowgirls on this cattle drive range in age from 6 to 11, and hardly a foot out of the entire bunch reaches the stirrups on their roping saddles.

"Good job!" Tiffany says after only a few more minutes, when the cattle are inside the pen. "See, you have to do it as a team; you can't do it alone."

When she asks if anyone wants to head to the shade of the barn for a break from the scorching sun, the group unanimously opts to move the herd around the arena again.

This was the scene from the Davis Rodeo Camp at the Davis Ranch in Archdale, North Carolina in June. A week later, an older group, ages 12-16, was there to learn horsemanship and rodeo skills.

Rodeo and bull-riding fans will likely recognize Davis Rodeo Company and its signature brand, the Diamond D. Tiffany and her husband, former professional bull rider Jerome Davis, run the company known for hosting Professional Bull Riding events, barrel races and other rodeo activities.

Davis Rodeo is also known for its quality bucking bulls. With a full breeding operation and several highly ranked bucking bulls, the Davises are on the road much of the year, hauling their stock to various rodeo events.

Jerome began making a mark in the rodeo world in 1990 when he won the titles of North Carolina state rodeo champion and national high school rodeo reserve all-around champion. Bull riding rocketed him to the apex at the national level and he remained in the top five in the world standings for most of the 1990s. In that time, he claimed winnings in excess of $1 million and captured bull riding's highest honor in 1995: world champion bull rider.

In 1998, a bull-riding accident left Jerome partially paralyzed and unable to compete but never diminished his love for rodeo. Jerome fully admits, "I knew that it was a dangerous sport." He faces that reality in a straightforward way, obviously underpinned with unwavering faith. Even after coping with such an extreme injury, his philosophy remains, "You gotta go with what hand you got dealt." Jerome is one to practice what he preaches.

This tenacious cowboy and his equally determined wife continued to work in the rodeo world. Tiffany's father had owned a regional rodeo company and, at the time of Jerome's accident, Tiffany and Jerome were already hosting rodeo events at the Davis Ranch.

After Jerome's accident, they rebounded and put their hearts into launching the Davis Rodeo Company. The enterprise has grown into a successful business, hosting many annual events including the North Carolina Christian Junior Rodeo and the Davis Rodeo Barrel

Racing Tour, which begins in April in Oak Ridge, North Carolina and continues for eight stops, ending in December at the Virginia Horse Center in Lexington, Virginia.

While the Davises are known for their bucking bulls, it's their American Quarter Horses who have been getting more of a workout lately.

"Hey cattle! Hey Cattle!" The youngsters get the swing of rounding up cattle with Tiffany coaching nearby. *(David Hart [www.hartphotos.us])*

Herding cattle is just one skill the young rodeo students develop at the Davis Rodeo Camp. When asked what their favorite part of the week is, the students answer unanimously "The HORSES!" Only then do the kids break it down into barrel racing, pole bending, rounding up the calves, roping, feeding the bulls and the ever popular outdoor summer rodeo activity—squirt-gun fights.

The excitement of these youngsters is contagious, and Jerome particularly loves that aspect of hosting the camps.

"I remember the first time I slick horned a dummy when I

was a kid," he shares, smiling. "I remember how excited I was, and it's great to give some of that back. It gets me excited to see these kids get excited! When they first showed up, most of them were scared to even get close to a horse, but by the end they were begging to lope around the arena."

The camp's horses all happen to be American Quarter Horses, most retired from barrel racing.

"They are just awesome," Tiffany says enthusiastically when asked about the breed's prominence in rodeo sports. "The Quarter [Horse] is just the backbone of rodeo."

Even though some of her barrel horses are well into their 20's, Tiffany still keeps a close eye on them. The 22-year-old sorrel gelding, "Boss," who traces to Three Bars (TB), has been with Tiffany since he was a yearling. He has a special place in her heart.

Usually a bit poky and great with kids, Boss occasionally has a sudden flashback to the many years of barrel racing competition he enjoyed with Tiffany. Noticing him pawing as a younger pupil sits on him preparing to take a slow trip around the barrel pattern, Tiffany walks briskly over to Boss and takes a hold on the reins.

"Boss goes from one extreme to the next," she says with a grin.

"When that other side comes out, you'd better hang on!" she explains, then walks the horse and rider around the barrels at a reasonable pace for a beginner.

Also working in the arena are several other retired barrel horses including Sonny Two Eyed Scout and Miss Bobby Brown.

In addition to barrel racing, pole bending and herding young cattle, the kids are responsible for the care of the horses. Their camp days begin with stall cleaning, feeding, watering and grooming. Then they saddle the horses. Along the way, the kids are taught how to properly tie the halter rope with a "quick release" knot, to not wrap the lead ropes around their hands, and how to approach, handle and mount a horse safely.

Later, the kids untack their horses and hose them off, and often themselves as well, before returning their new friends to their stalls. For most of the youngsters, this is the first opportunity to be entirely hands-on and responsible for horses and take part in rodeo activities.

The idea for the camp evolved naturally from the state of affairs on the Davis Ranch, Tiffany explains.

"The neighbors' kids used to stay around here in the summer time. I kept about five kids around here all the time and they loved it. I love kids. So that started the idea. Last year was my first camp, and we had 18 kids. They were everywhere, so I decided we had to cut it back and have two sessions. So we're just growing. Later on, if it keeps growing, we'll add more."

For more information on the Davis Rodeo Camps,
call (336) 861-ROPE or visit www.jeromedavis.com.

CHAPTER 3

Gwynn Turnbull Weaver.
(Emily Kitching [www.eclectic-horseman.com])

"WOMEN OF THE WEST:"
GWYNN TURNBULL WEAVER

This interview with Gwynn Turnbull Weaver ran in the May 2007 issue of Western Horseman in the "Women of the West" column. The full pre-edited draft, a slightly longer version of the interview, is provided here. Gwynn began the Californios Ranch Roping and Stock Horse Contest with her husband, Dave Weaver, in 2000. These days it is held in Reno, Nevada each May. Info on the event, a schedule of the Weavers' clinics, and info on their available videos can be found at www.thecalifornios.com.

There are no excuses for poor horsemanship anymore. If you run out of the information you need to progress, go find it. If that's too much trouble, then God help you and anything you might ride.

The current criteria used when judging and placing competitions is not designed to measure the type of results experienced by the alternative training methods. Our competitions are only as good as the criteria being measured and evaluated.

The Californios was a great experiment into the nature of humanity and our relationships with our horses. The journey we embarked on with the show was exhausting. It had all of the elements of the great westward expansion of this country. The same naysayers at the journey's beginning, the same organizational struggles, and then the same heartbreaking desolation in the middle of the trip, starvation, injury, hopelessness. There were times when we just wanted to lay down and let the buzzards have the show. I'm not sure what kept us going. But we kept going. Of course, as soon as the terrain changed and the smell of money drifted in on the wind, we had the same old opportunists swooping in, trying to capitalize on all the sweat. I'm sure this is always true. The show has shown us the best in people and worst. I try to focus on the best in them.

Many say that the west is breaking up. I think that is a fatalist attitude. A few fence lines, a few laws and a few trends can't defeat the great American west. She is still out there, just as she was 100 years ago. The west is a state of mind. As long as we value the ethics that she fostered, she'll still be there. What's big about the west is what it does to a person's heart. That is what it's all about and that is what cannot be divided.

I think balance keeps us honest, instead of the other way around.

I try very hard to regard each person as an individual—regardless of age, gender, or experience. As long as they conduct themselves in a manner worthy of respect, I will treat them with respect, and if they don't, I won't. I strive to keep it that simple. It's how I'd like to be regarded.

To define is to divide, so I don't address gender specific issues. Action is a universal barometer. If you walk the walk—my world has been very fair.

Sadly, we can't legislate ethics or morality, we can only encourage it. In the horse show world, that means changing what we measure and reward in such a way that it can only be achieved through ethical and moral practices.

Technology is not something to be used against the living things that we raise—it should be used to fine tune our stock handling and allow us the time to make more sensitive, ethical choices while turning a profit. I believe the entire beef industry needs an overhaul. So many producers are still stuck in the old 1950's assembly line/mass production style of animal handling. The world has evolved since then.

All great cowboys are sensitive people. They have to be to accomplish the level of excellence they have achieved with livestock. If they are calloused, they might be good, but they will never be great. Working with cattle and horses requires a tremendous amount of sensitivity. You have to be aware and feeling all the time. That is a difficult thing to preserve when you are faced with the unbiased suffering that mother nature can inflict on living things. There are some things that should bother a person, no matter how many times they deal with it. If you lose the ability to feel, you're just never going to get that handy. End of story.

If you are waiting for hard core competitors to wake up one morning and all of a sudden be concerned with what is in it for the horse, don't hold your breath. I don't think I have all of the answers when it comes to what is wrong with the show world and how to fix it—I do know that it has fallen precariously out of balance and unless we make a shift to bring it back into balance, it will most certainly collapse.

As much as I am disgusted with the current competitive horse show world, I don't think it should go away. That would be throwing the baby out with the bath water.

Accomplishing something with a horse in today's competitive world should not have to be at the horses expense all the time. Yes, there are times we ask a great deal of our horses, but there should be an equal number of times that they ask a great deal from us to bring things into balance. That might mean going against our ego and our pocketbook and doing the right thing for the horse from time to time.

We enjoy doing our clinics very much. If that ever changes, we'll hang it up. We work hard to balance out the kind of work we do. We only do about 15 clinics a year. This allows us time to find work on ranches, taking care of cattle, practicing what we preach. We feel that we need that, though the pay isn't very good. We would like to do clinics in the early spring and fall and care for some cattle on grass in our area in the winter. This allows me the opportunity to work on "The Californios" as it approaches in April.

We are also looking for a two month summer camp job in the high country up on top of the Big Horns in Wyoming, or something like that. We'll just have to see what comes available. I'd like to chronicle our summer camp job in a book. Try to let folks in on the experience from my point of view. I'm excited about that. I'm 44 this year—old enough to offer an interesting perspective, young enough to still do it.

Not everyone who likes horses should own or ride them, yet everyone who owns and rides them should like them.

I'm a person who always looks for meaning in things, the "why" is very important to me. I feel it is the barometer that keeps us all on course, evolving along in a positive way, a way that makes us better people, more balanced, more sensitive, more able to contribute something beneficial to the world at large. I don't mean everyone should be saving the world with some grand scheme, but I do believe that everyone doing just a little something, be it ever so humble, along the way will collectively benefit us all. I don't think that is unreasonable to expect from folks.

Of all the things I'll have to accept in my life, I pray silently that God will never let me know the last time I ride a horse.

Chapter 4

Dr. Bibb dressed in a tuxedo for his daughter's wedding.
(Susan Bibb)

Tribute to Dr. Bibb

Dr. Bibb was our large animal vet for a number of years. I wrote this essay shortly after his death in March 2006. The essay ran in the July 2011 issue of America's Horse magazine.

It wasn't quite 4:00 a.m. when I found out about Dr. Bibb. A friend, Terrie Wood, came by the farm here in southwest Virginia at 3:00 a.m. to pick me up and take me to Greensboro, N.C. to catch a flight to Phoenix. I drove as we crossed the Blue Ridge Parkway and wound down Tuggles Gap on a road that descends a quick thousand feet. The green glow of the dash lights revealed Terrie with her arms folded under her head, leaning against the window. I figured she was asleep, but suddenly she sat up and said, "Oh . . . did I tell you Dr. Bibb died?"

"What? He did not!" was my reaction. It wasn't possible . . . I'd just spoken to him earlier the day before. My mule Cate was a relative newcomer to the farm, and Dr. Bibb said he'd come out to check on a stiff leg she had and immunize the horses when I returned from my trip.

Terrie's housemate is a vet from another clinic, so she had gotten the news within hours of it happening, and while there weren't many details at that point for her to convey—it, unfortunately, did prove to be true.

At the top of Tuggles Gap, in the middle of nowhere just off the Blue Ridge Parkway, is Tuggles Gap Restaurant. It was eerie that Terrie popped up right past there to give me this news. One day as I worked on an article at my desk at home, the phone rang. It was an old friend, Sherry Baker, part owner of that restaurant. Dr. Bibb and I had spoken about Sherry a little over the past few months. He confided in me that she had a Thoroughbred colt that was in training at a racetrack in Arizona that he had worked on to overcome an issue in a rear leg. The three-year-old seemed to be doing well, but Sherry wanted to keep the whole thing quiet. The colt's official name, I learned, was Just Bibb's Brat. He had earned the title by being cantankerous with the old vet, and it showed the depth of the esteem the younger woman held for him, as well.

Sherry called because she knew I wrote about horses for a living and that I knew Dr. Bibb pretty well—and she had a crazy request. Out of the blue she explained she wanted to fund a documentary film on Dr. Bibb. She feared his stories, and his unique ways as a country vet (ones that seemed to be dying out in this modern world), would be lost if they weren't captured. The vet was approaching his seventies but still worked full time and seemed strong and healthy. Sherry was so deeply moved by his ways, however, that she was willing to take on the formidable obstacles of such an enterprise as the film to preserve what she could of him for the future while there still was time. I wasn't sure what this had to do with me until she asked if I would ride with him to get down what I could. She had apparently strong-armed him into agreeing to this deal, feeling that I would be the perfect candidate—a guy that knew him with a background in writing—and even invested in some digital recording equipment to get going. Of course I agreed. Heck, I'd wanted the opportunity to ride around with him and get some of his stories down for years. I'd even hinted at it to Dr. Bibb on several occasions myself.

But, we hadn't got the project going yet. There wasn't time. Now, what we both feared could be lost was gone. Now there truly was no longer time. I drove down Tuggles Gap thinking of so many "ifs" in the hours before dawn that day.

I thought about that last conversation I had with Dr. Bibb and about him in general quite a lot as I spent the next two weeks living in the front quarters of a four-horse trailer in the Arizona desert and learning from horsemanship clinician Harry Whitney. My emotions were amplified in that alien landscape (I'd never been out west before) with its barren ground, unreal and forever changing spectrum of sky colors, and visibility that only ends when blocked by a mountain range or where the curvature of the planet's surface dips below the sight line.

Things occurred to me about Dr. Bibb as I reflected then. Like how even though his first name was Thomas (I'm not even sure how I know this fact, now that I think of it), I never heard anyone ever, even long time friends of the same age group (he was 69), refer to him by any way other than "Dr. Bibb"—including himself. "Hello, this is Dr. Bibb," he always presented himself on the phone, even on his cell phone voice mail message. The image came to me of him hanging around one of the rural convenience stores drinking coffee and telling stories to a group of folks that inevitably gathered to hear

Dr. Bibb on the job.
(Susan Bibb)

the tales . . . all of them true. (Oh, if I could have recorded those chance meetings what material would be recorded!) I used to kid him and call these places his "satellite offices." Many times I'd be passing by one, see his truck parked out front, and stop in for an unscheduled appointment. It was a terribly effective way of getting good vet care at the spur of the moment.

As I acclimated to strange new tasks like plucking cactus needles from horses' pasterns, my wife Carol kept me updated, via cell phone, on the details of the funeral and the many conversations she had with folks in the community about our loss. She relayed that Dr. Bibb died suddenly from heart failure, working in Wytheville, Virginia. It seemed fitting in a way, that his last moments were spent vetting large animals. And, when I thought about that, it didn't take long for the full weight of what was lost with Dr. Bibb to begin bearing on my mind.

When I returned home two weeks later, everyone I came across in the community echoed the same sentiment, "We don't know what we're gonna do now that Dr. Bibb's gone . . . how 'bout you?"

"I don't know either," I replied. "Carol and I just aren't sure what to do."

Sure, there is the problem of finding another vet for the horses. Given the limitations of geography, there are only a few choices for large animal vets in the area. But, Dr. Bibb had been our only large animal vet since we moved to southwestern Virginia over a decade ago, and it was a relationship of absolute trust that couldn't be easily replaced. However, as big a thing as that was for us, I realized from talking to some friends who are farmers that Dr. Bibb had been the only vet several had ever used in their entire lives. That's one vet in nearly forty years. What a fact! What a true cornerstone a vet can be in the foundation of a rural community.

But the loss ran far deeper than just getting the large animals basic vet care. There is that anticipation of the future emergency. Dr. Bibb was the living embodiment of much veterinary knowledge, certainly well read and educated and active in a battalion of organizations that kept him up-to-date on the latest, but more importantly, he was likely unequalled in that other type that is gleaned from experience in the field of practice. He was so practical, so down-to-earth—and that was the huge problem we all now grappled with. Dr. Bibb made us all realize how things can be with a vet. I used to tell Carol, "if anything ever happens to me, call Dr. Bibb." The funny part is that I wasn't kidding—I'd trust him over a medical doctor any day, and you could get him. I think there's not a client of his that doesn't miss how getting advice or treatment was so simple, so practical, such a common sense/straightforward relationship with him. None of us knew who to try or just what to expect. We all were anticipating that never again would we enjoy such a pragmatic relationship with our vet.

To get Dr. Bibb, you dialed his cell phone. He either answered or called you back pretty quickly. If you needed advice, he'd talk through things with you on the phone. He was not quick to order some barrage of expensive tests, to send your livestock to the veterinary hospital, or even necessarily come out. He seemed to have an instinctual ability to read people and thereby know what condition their horse was in from a simple conversation with them. I had a wide range of reasons for calling him over the years; many where I was very concerned about the condition of one horse or another, and Dr. Bibb's advice to "wait and see" was undeniably the right choice. Then again, I have had very serious situations, like my colt Whipper Snapper tearing his eye, and without needing to come out and see what it looked like, Dr. Bibb had things lined up with Virginia Tech Vet Hospital before I even had the trailer connected. He knew. And he was right.

The medications he prescribed and provided were so cheap compared to other places, I'm not even sure he added any markup at all. I would even get de-wormer and fly repellent from him because it was so affordable. And, I noticed a long time ago, that it costs three times more for me to drive one of my dogs to the small animal vet for an in-clinic visit than to get Dr. Bibb to come out and check three horses and a mule in the field. Why is that? The man proved by how he lived his life and ran his practice that the world can make some sense. That vets can be accessible and affordable. I'm sure that's part of the tribute to Dr. Bibb that Sherry wanted to make and to preserve for future generations.

I suppose once we all deal with the loss of a friend, the loss of a capable vet, and the loss of a great story teller, that we are left with the daunting task of trying to fill the void created by his passing. I'm extremely grateful to have known him and to be part of that group that will understand just what is meant when people reference his name, though it has made the task of finding a replacement all the more difficult. I suppose it's just as difficult on those poor vets who must fill the void and endure the knowledge that they are scrutinized and evaluated on the "Bibb scale."

CHAPTER 5

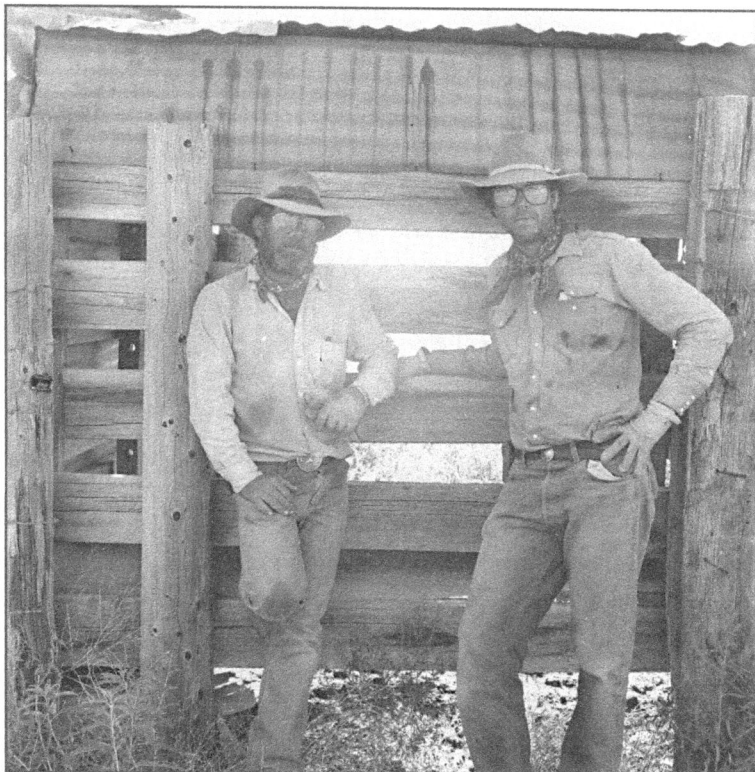

Douglas Preston and Walter Nelson find a little shade in the desert
as they pursue Coronado deeper into North America.
(Walter Nelson [www.walterwnelson.com])

IN THE HOOF PRINTS OF CORONADO

*Researching and writing the first article in this book on David
O'Connor's horseback journey from Maryland to Oregon captivated my interest*

in "equestrian travel." Not trail riding, not endurance riding, but another kind of journey made horseback. A journey ridden across hundreds, thousands, or occasionally even tens of thousands of miles. Not a race, but a personal trek out in the world. Riders and their horses setting a course for the horizon and hitting the road at a few miles an hour, enduring any number of hardships along the way that would be easily alleviated by simply hopping in a climate controlled vehicle and zipping along the highway at seventy-five miles an hour.

I was very fortunate to interview two men who made one of the craziest long rides ever in North America: Walter Nelson and Douglas Preston. This article ran in the July 2008 issue of Horse Connection magazine: www.horseconnection.com. Preston is a successful author of numerous novels and has co-written many others with Lincoln Child. More information on him is available at: www.prestonchild.com. Nelson is an accomplished photographer and artist. He currently is the Director of The Abiquiu Workshops at Ghost Ranch in New Mexico: www.abiquiuworkshops.com.

"I was a complete dude," admits long rider and acclaimed writer Douglas Preston. Given his accomplishment, it is a truth difficult to believe.

Without previous horseback experience, a 1,000 mile brutal, middle-of-nowhere, get-yourself-killed, deserts-of-the-American-southwest long ride became Preston's hellacious introduction to the saddle. The year was 1989.

The modern day long ride through the desolate desert region from near the Mexican border of Arizona to Santa Fe, New Mexico firmly established Preston in the ranks of the Long Riders' Guild, an international association of equestrian Argonauts who hail from 38 countries. Each LRG member completed a continuous horseback journey of 1,000 miles or more. Likewise, his adventuresome equine endeavor was again internationally recognized when he was made a Fellow of the Royal Geographical Society.

Even among such notable company, this long rider's expedition ranks highly in the categories of sheer physical near-impossibility and historical significance. It is especially remarkable given the journey's location and time frame of the latter 20th century, when North American horsemanship underwent previously unparalleled voluntary confinement to popular indoor arenas and round-pens as opposed to seeking challenging rides to horizons hundreds of miles distant.

The inspiration for this equestrian trek was the documentation of its history. In 1540, a Spaniard, Francisco Vázquez de Coronado, led the first European expedition into the heart of what became America in search of the fabled "seven cities of gold." Coronado amassed 300 Spanish soldiers, more than 1,000 Tlaxcalac Indians, and a sizable herd of livestock and led the expedition north from Mexico into the unforgiving desert land of the southwest.

That historical long ride was the first to penetrate deep into the American interior by Europeans. Historians have expended furious energy and considerable quantities of ink over its details for centuries. The expedition encountered several sizable Indian settlements, though none glittering of gold as reputed. The journey was thus a failure in the eyes of the Spanish. It remains, however, one of the world's all time major cultural crossroads. It was the flash-point at which Europeans and many Native American societies made first contact. Horses, having disappeared from North America for thousands of years, were reintroduced to this part of the globe by Coronado's expedition. The continent's radical alteration and race to the modern era in essence was sparked by this event.

The second documented long ride through the country that Coronado first explored was initiated by the mind that later produced such celebrated thrillers as *Relic* and *Tyrannosaur Canyon*. For Douglas Preston, riding this route ultimately would help ignite that distinguished career as a *New York Times* best selling author. It also provided for his equestrian education and fashioned him as a horseman in a gritty, seriously old school, hombre way.

Preston set out to experience first-hand what the earlier horseback expedition encountered. It proved an easy task, since that country remains virtually unchanged since Coronado's time—it is every bit as inhospitable, barely penetrable in places, short of water, and extremely deadly.

"I wanted to write a book about Coronado," Preston says. "I just didn't feel I was getting the real history. I wasn't getting the grit of it. I wanted to write a book that would capture it. The problem with historians is that they don't get out and do it. They haven't experienced it. These professors who wrote about Coronado knew absolutely nothing about horses or the terrain."

At the beginning, Preston was himself a New England writer and researcher (that's bookworm, not seasoned equestrian adventurer). Working too many hours for too many years inside the American Museum of Natural History in New York City inspired him to get out there and make the ride to better know for certain just what must have happened. He struck out from the concrete confines of that academic crypt with all his worldly belongings piled in a Subaru and drove to sunny Santa Fe, New Mexico, following, he says, the advice of S. J. Perelman that "the dubious privilege of a freelance writer is he's given the freedom to starve anywhere."

Walter Nelson packed this Deardorf camera and its supplies for the entire 1,000 journey. *(Walter Nelson [www.walterwnelson.com])*

Starvation circled him like a buzzard out west, sure enough, but on his horseback adventure it proved to be one of the more trivial predicaments he encountered. The journey nearly killed him and the traveling companion he talked into accompanying him, distinguished western photographer Walter Nelson, a dozen times at least. And then there were the difficult parts of the journey.

"The hard part isn't riding," Preston reflects, "the hard part is when you're not riding."

Where does one tie a horse when there is nothing but barren earth from horizon to horizon, for example? One cannot ride a horse endlessly in general, let alone in hot, dry desert conditions. There were times when they had to stop and rest, consoling themselves with no certainty of water ahead in the near future. Of course, no roads or feed stores dotted the area . . . nothing was there but perhaps a few predators, the stars, and thorny, scruffy brush to keep them company while they sat in the dust hoping to make it somewhere for the next drink and meal suitable for horses primarily, and humans if lucky.

Somehow, rather than becoming a sun burnt pile of bones in one of the most remote places on earth (as predicted by several seasoned cowboys from the area), the men completed the long ride and Preston was transformed. Incredibly, he had no previous horseback experience when he set out to complete as difficult a journey as North America has to offer. The writer, while in the saddle all day every day, soon became a horseman . . . and it's a good thing, as there existed no escape route or life raft from this adventure.

Like Coronado in 1540, no golden cities awaited Preston in 1989, but he did discover some nuggets of truth out in the desert. Preston recorded information about many factors of the route, such as geography and availability of water, that directly relate to horseback travel. These provided new insights into understanding which routes could or could not have been taken and how things likely went for a sizable mounted expedition in the same area centuries earlier. In places where Coronado's exact route has been uncertain to scholars for centuries, Preston's new insights provide a very high probability of which way was taken. It becomes clear as a practical matter discernable in the field with a horse, rather than an endless circular debating of routes on maps spread over a table under fluorescent lights, or even from an air conditioned SUV on a road overlooking a small part of the bleak route.

Preston's new equestrian based skills and findings merged with his existing academic abilities. Upon completion of the journey he wrote the definitive book on Coronado's famous first long ride entitled, *Cities of Gold*. It is the only first-hand modern account of horseback travel on the conquistador's route. The only other texts were those surviving from the original journey, penned mostly by a member of the expedition named Pedro de Castaneda.

"Many historians have gone right on writing about Coronado since *Cities of Gold* came out but have completely ignored it," Preston says, chuckling. "Horses don't fit with their lifestyles. They tend to be sedentary people. They are very judgmental of what Coronado did [violent encounters in particular] not taking into account the desperation for food and for food for their horses."

Coronado wasn't the only trail blazer beckoning Preston into a saddle in the desert southwest.

"I was definitely inspired by Clyde Kluckhohn at Harvard," Preston explains. "As a young man he made this ride back in the 20s to the Rainbow Bridge."

The ride Preston refers to is immortalized in the book, *To the Foot of the Rainbow*, written by Kluckhohn, (published by LRG Press: www.horsetravelbooks.com). Kluckhohn became a preeminent professor of anthropology in America in the mid-20th century, but as a young New Englander convalescing in the arid climate of the American west, his curiosity drove him into the saddle for a historical long ride. Much like Preston, from the east and without equestrian experience, he saddled up and headed into the unforgiving desert on adventure. Kluckhohn sought a legendary natural stone bridge that reputedly existed on Navajo lands. He became one of the first white men to ride to the remote sight and see the incredible rock formation.

"Kluckhohn was my father's professor," Preston explains of their personal connection. "My father majored in anthropology;

that's how I came to know about him. I read the book."

Preston has continued to ride since his initial horseback experience in 1989. In 1993 he took another long ride. This one 400 miles across Navajo territory in Utah and New Mexico along the Moonlight Trail with his fiancée, Christine, and her daughter, Selene. It is the basis for another book, *Talking to the Ground: One Family's Journey on Horseback Across the Sacred Land of the Navajo*, published in 1995 by Simon & Schuster.

Preston says he has taken many other trips on horseback and prefers going out for at least a hundred miles or so. These days, he and his son, Isaac, take to the trails around the New Mexico region where the family has a rustic bit of property.

"Even if you know a lot about horses," he says, "you're not necessarily ready for something like a long ride. The old ways, like hobbling, are critical. We [Nelson and Preston] had to re-invent or re-discover some of the old ways. Most people saddle up, go riding, and come back to the barn."

"I have found that feeding horses on a rigid schedule is not a good way to prepare a horse for a long ride," he gives as an example on the LRG website (www.thelongridersguild.com), "when they might be turned out to graze at any time of the day or night or given feed at unexpected hours. Riding in the desert, you never know when you're going to come across a beautiful patch of grass or when you're going to pass by a ranch where you can buy oats. If you feed a horse on a rigid schedule he will be much more likely to colic when his feeding schedule is disrupted on the trail. What's worse, a horse fed on a strict schedule becomes highly anxious on the trail when the feed times are delayed or changed or when there isn't enough feed. So I try to alter feeding times and, once in a while, I actually skip a feeding time.

"I do several other things with horses that I feel are essential to make a good long-rider horse, but which might not be usual for most horse lovers. In the wild, horses tend to drink twice a day, in the morning and at evening. It is good to train a horse to do without water, so they learn to drink well (but not over or under drink) when water is available. So at home, I let the horses only water twice a day and do not give them free, all-day-long access to water. On the trail, the horse does not get anxious or panicky at not having water all day, and when we do find water (I've done a lot of desert long-distance riding) the horse knows that he should drink well when he has the chance."

Douglas Preston and Redbone, his favorite mount from the trip. *(Walter Nelson [www.walterwnelson.com])*

Preston recognizes that the mainstream horse world now, like today's horse magazines, are, "oriented for people who ride around in the ring or arena." It simply isn't a world he finds appealing.

"I did a bit of riding with Indians as well," he continues. "Navajo mostly. They're my kind of riders. Many bareback or on crappy saddles and on horses with conformational defects. But the Navajos have a sense of fun. We would ride like hell through the country. These horses and riders share a sense of wildness.

"That's my style of riding. All that stuff that I can't stand, I think it crushes the spirit of the horse."

Side Bar: Walter Nelson

"Doug called up one day and said, 'How'd you like to go on a trip with me?'" explains Walter Nelson about the beginning's of their extraordinary long ride. "We just took off."

Nelson possessed certain qualities recognized by his neighbor in New Mexico, Douglas Preston, that made him a good candidate for going on the onerous excursion he proposed of following in

Coronado's hoof prints. Nelson was a well known photographer and artist possessing a certain openness of mind, he had the guts to press onwards when others slunk back or laughed at the prospect of the journey, and growing up in Texas (and unlike Preston) he at least had a decent familiarity with horses. These proved essential aspects for the success of the journey that gained him a place among other tenacious adventurers who have earned membership in the Long Riders' Guild.

One of the most amazing aspects of this historical equestrian adventure through the unforgiving southwest desert southwest was that Nelson documented it in photographs—not just any photographs snapped with a typical camera. Think more along the lines of Ansel Adams. Nelson brought along a pack horse for the task of hauling a Deardorf 8" x 10" camera, tripod, and the large format film along for the entire 1,000 mile adventure. With the age of digital technology upon us, this endeavor deep into the remote southwest may be the last to capture such images onto silver or platinum film plates.

"I had a sawbuck pack saddle," he explains. "I had special saddle bags made out of high density foam padding and white tarpaulin that truckers use."

Nelson customized the pack saddle to hold the delicate gear and also covered the equipment when packed on the horse with a shiny metallic "space blanket." This material reflected the heat of the 100+ degree days and insulated the film and photographic equipment as much as possible. For the horse, it was surely a nice trade-off for packing the gear, as well.

"It [the space blanket] got shredded," he says of one challenge that began early on. "From the start we went through curtains of green and brown—it was cat's claw and mesquite."

Nelson, now 65, bought the camera in New York City in 1981 when he worked there as a professional photographer.

"I just believe in doing things bigger," he says, laughing about the burden of taking a hundred pounds of photographic gear into such a scorching and dusty place and over so many miles. He adds, "It was my primary camera for years and years. If you want to go into the landscape and photograph the landscape, the amount of information because of the size of the negative, 8" x 10," is 50 times greater than a 35 mm camera—1" x 1 ½". Your resolution doesn't fall apart [in the printed image] . . . it holds together. A black and white silver print is so much more beautiful."

Changing around the extremely light sensitive film into different compartments of the pack was no small challenge on the trip. Nelson would wait until dark. Even then on the clear moonless desert nights, starlight was bright enough to affect the film. Preston had a tent onto which Nelson piled tarps, and then he would enter with the gear to quickly swap film around.

"Smithsonian underwrote the project," Nelson explains of the long ride. They published numerous images he made on the journey with the Deardorf, which accompanied an article written by Preston. "It was a wonderful spread," he says.

Recently, Nelson and Preston collaborated on another project, a book entitled, *Ribbons of Time*. The book is a portrait of a single, little known canyon in the Big Bend area of Texas which combines Nelson's photography and Preston's text.

For information on the book or other artistic and photographic works by Nelson visit: www.walternelson.com.

CHAPTER 6

Dutch Lunak working as a stunt double for Buffalo-
Hump during the filming of *Comanche Moon.*
(Sled Reynolds)

DUTCH LUNAK–HOLLYWOOD WRANGLER

*The following article originally ran in the August 2010 issue of
America's Horse magazine (www.AQHA.com). Dutch is an incredible*

character, and I've written another article on his veteran "lay down" stunt horse, Crackers, for Paint Horse Journal. I also interviewed his wife, Ann, for Western Horseman's "Women of the West" department; an extended version of that interview is the next chapter in this book.

If you've seen a major film or TV western featuring both Indians and horses in the past two decades, then you've likely seen the work of Hollywood wrangler and stunt man, Alvin "Dutch" Lunak and some of his American Quarter Horses. Lunak owns Ghostridge Outfitters, a movie wrangling and Quarter Horse breeding business based in Valier, Montana.

"We're up here on the Blackfeet Indian reservation on the Canadian border," Lunak says. "I'm a Blackfeet, Chippewa affiliated. I was raised right here across the creek from our property on my grandfather's place."

Lunak has wrangled horses and worked as a stunt double for over twenty years. Around 40 Hollywood feature films and TV movies are on his resume, including *Dances with Wolves, The Last of the Mohicans, Hidalgo, 3:10 to Yuma, Comanche Moon,* and *Appaloosa.*

Lunak and his brother, Scotty Augare, got started together working in the movies in the late 1970s.

"We got started wranglin' when they came up to the reservation here to do a movie called *War Party*," Lunak explains. "It's been, oh, twenty-five years ago. I'd messed my knee up, so I wasn't riding bucking horses at the time. Sled Reynolds [a long established Hollywood wrangler and animal trainer] came up and they had kind of a tryout thing. I had a gray heeling horse, a roping horse, I took him in there and rode him. They liked the looks of the horse—they didn't say much about me—so they asked if I'd bring the horse up to the director the next day to look at for one of the actors, Kevin Dillan. So, I took my horse up there. In the meanwhile we're standing around there, and the actors were there, and I was the exact size of Kevin Dillan. So, they asked me to stunt double for him. They didn't use my horse for the movie, but they asked me to be a riding double for him, so that's how I got started."

The first step when making a movie that involves horses, Lunak explains, is filling the position of Head Wrangler. Once that slot is filled, he establishes his wrangling crew and sets about the task of finding the right horses for the necessary roles in the film. It may be as specific as a black horse that rears on cue, or a sorrel that lays down. Whatever the needs, the wranglers find horses for the parts and begin training them well in advance for the particular situation that will be required during filming.

"I'm mostly brought in by other wranglers," Lunak says. "I've been a stunt coordinator and a stunt man and then a wrangler, too. Some movies I do all three. The show, *3:10 to Yuma*, we had quite a few Quarter Horses out of our stud there—our stud [Check The Prisoners] is out of Streakin Six, who is one of the top running horses in the United States, comes from the Four-Sixes ranch down there in Texas. For the posse that was in that movie, Russell Crowe was the main actor, and he had a group of bad guys with him. We furnished all the horses for his gang. Rusty Hendrickson was the head wrangler and he asked us to bring the horses for the posse, a couple of doubles, and I brought a horse that lays down."

Horse wrangling for movies is a huge responsibility, according to Lunak. Other jobs on a movie set may start and stop at certain times of the day or allow days off. Horses, however, are kept close by during filming and require regular basic care everyday. Additionally, they must be well trained and rehearsed for certain tricks or scenes. Then, of course, there is working with the horses during the filming itself. Pre-production for movies can start from six weeks to three months ahead of filming. The movie wrangler depends on this time for finding and preparing just the right horses for all the various scenes.

"I've never left a movie set," Lunak admits, "because when you get on one, you've got ten or twelve horses there . . . you just don't leave. And you get certain actors and you get them on your horses and they're still relying on you to be there everyday to help them through different scenes. It's probably about eighty percent teaching an actor, whether it's a main actor or all the way down to the extra that's working the day—making them feel comfortable, making it look like they know what they're doing when they actually don't. It's almost like being a coach. So you get somebody you've never met before, and the head wrangler tells you: 'you take so-and-so over there, and today he has to run through this gully here, turn around, shooting back.' You take the individual actor over, you get him used to the horse, then you start teaching him how you would do that particular job."

All the fancy tricks horses are seen doing in films may seem like really tough training jobs. According to Lunak, though, one of the greatest difficulties a wrangler faces on set may come as a surprise.

"One of the hardest things with a horse that's a rodeo horse, or a horse that's done something else like run on a track, is to get them to stand there while they're setting the cameras up, and then delivering the dialogue. You know, you don't want them jiggling around or moving around. A lot of it is just getting that horse

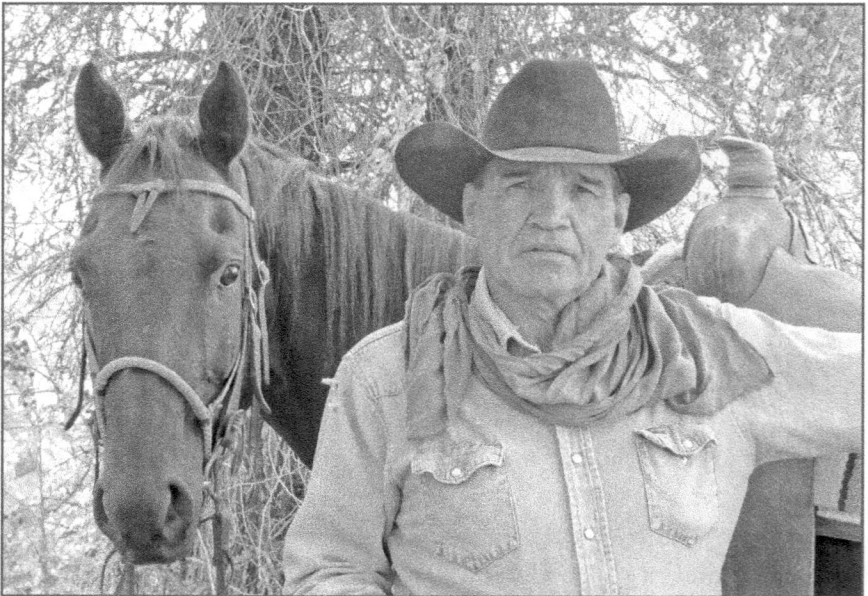

Dutch Lunak with his special "lay-down" horse, Crackers. (Ann Lunak)

changing his whole way of thinking and his whole way of life. That horse is used to running at barrels full bore, pole bending—then take him down there and make him stand for fifteen or twenty minutes with a green actor . . . it's challenging!

"Really the most appealing thing for me about the film industry is seeing how different trainers and wranglers do different things. What I've been able to do over the years by working with some of the best trainers in Hollywood in the horse business, you know—Rex Peterson, Rusty Hendrickson, Sled Reynolds—is being able to pick up some of the things that fit into my work. Some things don't work too good for me, and then a lot of things I've picked up over the years really have helped, not only with training our film horses, but also with the everyday saddle horses and rodeo horses. There's no boundaries to what you can learn when you work with the top trainers in any business."

One big challenge of being a movie wrangler, Lunak points out, is the time it requires being away from home. Since a typical movie shoot lasts for several months, some even longer, and the wrangling responsibilities make it nearly impossible to leave, his wife, Ann, and daughters, Megan and Jimi, sometimes visit him when he is working on a film. Not only has Lunak traveled the United States to work on films, but he also went to Mexico, and even to Namibia in Africa for eight months to work on the film, *Running Free*. Leaving home with its responsibilities of horses and cattle that run on more than two thousand acres of northern Montana, is no simple thing.

"I've been gone so much some years, I've never even hardly seen our cows," Lunak says. "We've run anywhere from about two hundred and fifty to three hundred cows, and from twenty to two hundred head of horses at a time over the years. They'd [the family] have to winter them. They'd have to get them in in the spring and brand the calves. Take them to summer pasture. Ride on them all summer. And then that fall gather them up. We run them up in the mountains here on the reservation, up in the Rocky Mountains. Ship our calves . . . my wife teaches school. It's kind of a trying time, but really a team effort with my family. It took a lot of effort from a lot of people so that I could go. An extended family is a nice thing."

Lunak is retired from stunt work now. Recommendations, however, continue to carry over into his wrangling business. Indian movies in particular are his forte, he says. These days Ghostridge Outfitters gets called upon to coordinate larger groups of Native American riders along with horses for movies that need them.

"At the end of the day," Lunak says of his success in the film industry, "you get your job completed and your boss is happy with you . . . well, they'll call you back. Or ask for your horse. Or at least give you a good recommendation on another show. My whole movie career has been made off recommendations. We're way up here out of Hollywood and out of the movie scene, so by the time we hear about a movie they're pretty much into 'crew-up.' One particular wrangler that really helped us out over the years was Rudy Ugland. He did a lot of the big Indian movies, like *Geronimo: American Legend* and *Son of the Morning Star.*"

Lunak and his family breed, raise, train, and use American Quarter Horses in movie work for definite reasons. It is easy to get Lunak talking about how he came to know the breed, which was not around the reservation when he was young.

"I'm 57 years old, and I started breaking and riding colts when I was probably eight years old. Over the course of the years I've seen the Quarter Horse start coming into our herds. There's very little buck in those horses. There's no meanness in them. There's no comparison to the horses I learned how to break. With that Streakin Six line, we like to say that they're almost born broke, and I say that a lot with our horses we raise now.

"You don't have to put really hard pressure on them. They're versatile. We can take a Quarter Horse, break him to ride, take him on a movie, throw harness on him and three or four days he's pulling a wagon. You can put a little kid on him. You can put actors on that have never been on a horse and trust that that horse isn't gonna run off . . . you just couldn't do that with the horses I was raised riding.

"That's the biggest part of the American Quarter Horse that we have today, particularly our Streaking Six stud, is that their offspring are so trusting. That makes our job a lot more easy. We can turn our horses out for six months, get them in, clean them up, get on them, and ride them off like they'd been rode yesterday. You know, they're that type of horse."

"Dutch" and Ann Lunak
Ghostridge Outfitters
Wrangling and American Quarter Horses
302 Badger Creek
Valier, Montana 59486
(406) 338-2383
(406) 450-0668 cell

CHAPTER 7

Ann Lunak. *(Tony Bynum [www.tonybynum.com])*

"WOMEN OF THE WEST:"
ANN LUNAK

Ann Lunak's interview ran in the March 2011 issue of Western Horseman. The story re-printed here is the longer original draft I turned in before the final cuts were made for the magazine's space requirements, which includes a few previously unpublished quotes.

Ann Lunak was born in Kansas. She was still a toddler when her father moved north and settled on the Blackfeet Reservation in Montana to ranch, a stone's throw from the Canadian border. After college she married her high school sweetheart, Alvin "Dutch" Lunak, a Blackfeet Indian rancher and prominent Hollywood horse wrangler and stunt double. For more than two decades based from their ranch in Valier, Montana, they've run Ghostridge Outfitters providing horses and riders for feature and TV films, bred registered American Quarter Horses, run a cattle ranch, raised rodeo bucking horses, and raised two girls—Megan and Jimi, now in their twenties. Aside from teaching school full time, Ann runs the ranch when Dutch is away with movie work.

Our summer pasture is on the east slope of the Rocky Mountains, called the "backbone of the world" by Blackfeet. Our winter range is to the east in the fertile grain country on the Blackfeet Reservation. We use a lot of horse trailers and a lot of ranch horses. The land is primarily leased through the Bureau of Indian Affairs, available to Native Americans like my husband, Dutch, who is a Blackfeet/Chippewa.

There weren't many dating options where I grew up. Town was an hour and a half away. My Dad would say that we were so far out that we had to buy our own tomcats. I was high school age . . . there were two guys: one was a kid from across the border with a tractor, the other was a good looking cowboy who rode the south ridge on a pretty horse—I took the horse!

The west is changing, but here it's changing at a much slower pace than you might find off the reservation. The western horse culture here is alive and well. Since we're on the reservation, I think that urban sprawl is different in that you don't see Ted Turner types coming in and gobbling up large portions of land as much. It's more like families just wanting to settle on their own land and raise their own livestock, especially horses.

We've been doing the movie stuff twenty years, and we've been married for thirty-five. Sure there's more barbed wire fences. But still, we can ride our horses from our house to the mountains and maybe open one gate, and that's thirteen miles.

You walk a fine line between being responsible and being respectful to other ranchers. You have to be responsible and make sure that your business is done and that you're not causing somebody else trouble. You have to be responsible in that you get your cows home and make sure that other people get their cows home—and respectful to those who might not think that a woman should be riding out there with the men. I am sensitive to this perception at first, and then pretty soon I think that I become a part of the bigger picture of the job at hand, not just a woman.

I always remember that I'm not as handy as some men, so I'm not afraid to have a few key people in my corner that can help me. Dutch's family and friends are real cowboys, and I'm forever indebted to these guys. They're the kind I can call from a cell phone on top of a mountain in a snowstorm and say, "Where's the gate?" And they seem to know which fence line I need to follow and what draw I need to go down—I've done that before.

When we start gathering, it's an "old time" round up where we might get most of the cattle one time and then we go back up to get the stragglers as the fall storms drive them down to the prairie or the foothills, which is where we live. We hold them there until we have enough to truck or trail down to where the winter grazing—50 miles by the road or 35 miles as the crow flies. Then we ship calves at the end of November, which in Montana can be an experience.

One time I had a little bunch of pairs headed for the trail to the corral and I rode behind a new beaver dam. What a beautiful spot with golden aspen and red willows reflected in the still, dark water. I stopped to get a picture, and I lost my little bunch of cattle. They raced back up the mountainside. We didn't get that bunch for another month and barely in time to ship to market.

In May it's hurry up and wait! We're nearly out of hay by the first of May. The cattle are eagerly seeking the new but weak grass and walk away from hay. The farmers want us away from the farm ground, and the mountains aren't a place to be yet. The Blackfeet word for a killer storm in early spring is Maàk-appi. Three or four feet of wet snow dumped on young calves can, and has been, disaster.

Every time Dad [Dutch] would leave for a movie, everybody had to up a notch to the next level of family management. The girls were responsible for a lot but eventually grew into handy cowgirls. They were reminiscing [recently] about the glamour days when Dutch would be gone: cold feet that hurt when you stepped off a horse back at the barn; young horses that spooked when the wind would whip reins and overcoats; snow sifting and drifting above the backs of the cows and down your neck, and stubborn calves to suckle on a school night.

I could let myself be afraid to do things alone, but the more I step out and do things the more confident I feel. Sometimes when Dutch comes home, I might slip back into an easier, more comfortable role. I need to help him rather than just handing it over . . . going, "Shew! I'll go do something else!" There's not many things better than the sensation you feel when you've just finished a task that at first seemed impossible.

Ranching and raising horses comes with a sense of identity and a sense of pride. Our country has some smart and tough ladies. Dutch's aunt, a single lady, runs two thousand cattle. She's the matron of that ranch who knows the cattle business and is there every step of the way. She is my hero!

Sometimes people can appear to be a braggart and "cuss up wind." I don't think that image is as appealing as someone who has the image of being a lady, yet still responsible and somewhat capable.

In matters of dealing with death or illness in animals or people, a rancher doesn't get the luxury of taking time out. You need to be strong because you have to keep going. The animals don't know that you're having a hard day.

After the work is done, the men might hang out in the barn and talk. The women might talk cooking, a job in town, or kids and grand kids. But when it comes right down to the decisions and the work put in to making a ranch survive, the women are there right along with the men.

Sometimes I think men don't do so well without women. I think women tend to pass on the culture and those traditions that cycle through our lives and are so important. When we brand, are gathering cattle, or are calving, it's big meals and the traditions that surround those meals. The women might work outside all day, but still make time to slip those favorite dishes into the event. Calving comes with late night meals, Easter dinner at the calving barn, and an occasional birthday cake. Inside the house or outside with the animals, it's still the woman who seems to put those traditions in place.

I live in a very multi-cultural community, but I think that a horse culture seems to supersede gender and economic status . . . and that's a real powerful thing. The horse and ranch people are who you go sit with at the ball games and who you end up talking to at the store.

It's the people that you invite to your child's graduation or your wedding. It doesn't matter if you're on the movie set with Dutch's guys or at the rodeo or at the race track, wherever you are—school events—horse people tend to find each other. And maybe that's why I get by. I truly respect the horse people; I am lucky enough to be allowed to be a part of that.

CHAPTER 8

Barefoot trimmer, Terrie Wood, works on Niji.
(Carol Moates)

BAREFOOT TRIM
WHAT EXACTLY IS A BAREFOOT TRIM?

The idea of a "barefoot horse" with a specific "barefoot trim" entered my horsemanship vocabulary quite early on in my obsession with horses. The sudden and rather late onset of my passion for horses, in my mid-thirties, is well

*documented in my first horse book, Discovering Natural Horsemanship (The
Lyons Press, 2006). A chapter in that book is devoted to the topic of barefoot
horses. Even earlier, an article I wrote on barefoot trims was the cover feature of
the magazine Natural Horse (volume 6-issue 6), which ran in late 2004.*

*My understanding of hoof care (natural and otherwise) developed right
along with that of horsemanship (natural and otherwise) as the years progressed.
I even began trimming our horses, a job I never expected to undertake. The
article published here initially ran in the November 2008 issue of The American
Quarter Horse Journal. Its instigation was my desire to state the facts from
both barefoot trim and mainstream farrier professionals, accompanied by sound
veterinary advice.*

*It seemed to me, near-fanatical views held by some enthusiasts of both
sides of the hoof trim debate polarized the world of hoof care into various
camps. It became hard to navigate such splattered information, interests, and
advice. Confused equine caretakers, I thought, are not very helpful to horses.
This article was my attempt to provide trustworthy information and opinions from
two highly educated, experienced, and sensible hoof care experts in America: one
a professional natural hoof trimmer, and the other a certified farrier, vet, and a
celebrated expert on equine lameness.*

In the past several years the terms "barefoot" and "barefoot
trim" have come into wide usage on the horse scene. Barefoot, of
course, is hardly a new term to horse folk. It is self-explanatory and
has a long history of usage akin to "unshod." Lately, however, it has
developed a new connotation, much like the word "natural" in horse
lingo these days.

While a barefoot horse clearly always is one without shoes,
just exactly what constitutes a barefoot trim is less certain. Adding
to the confusion is a host of other terms under the barefoot trim
umbrella like "mustang trim," "natural trim," and "wild horse trim"
that also get tossed about frequently in this recent movement.

The equine hoof care landscape can be very puzzling and
enormously uncertain for a horse owner trying to figure out just what

it all really means. In the United States, anyone can decide to work as a farrier or trimmer, unlike in England for instance, where the trade is regulated by law similar to that of veterinary medicine. This means that in this country it is entirely the horse owner's responsibility to find a capable trimmer or farrier. Many highly qualified farriers self-regulate through organizations such as the American Farrier's Association (AFA) www.americanfarriers.org. The 2010 Alltech FEI World Equestrian Games recognized AFA farriers as the official qualified farriers of their event. Still, this well established group, which seeks to operate an association of professionals competent to both shoe and trim, often runs counter to many barefoot trimmers who reject the work of farriers wholesale.

So much buzz and quite a few claims of innovation in the realm of trims, without any central governing authority to help sort it out, leaves the horse owner vulnerable to hiring less capable or misguided trimmers. On the other hand, having a great deal of enthusiastic interest and study implemented to improve the vitally important area of equine hoof care provides a new awareness of trim variations. This also creates a more accessible range of choices to maximize hoof health, performance, longevity, and soundness. So, when you get down to it, what is this barefoot trim exactly anyway?

Variations abound in the use of these barefoot trimming terms, and the actual trims they denote may be just as varied as the people doing them. Often, the different names given to an assortment of trims are used like a trademark by some practitioners to assert a particular way of trimming, even if it is only a slight deviation from others. The barefoot trim, however, can be demystified.

Generally speaking, the idea of a barefoot trim is to attempt to mimic on domestic horses the kind of wear that it is thought they would experience if they were running in the wild on a relatively hard surface. The theory being that nature works out what's best for the horse in the wild, so humans should provide that natural design onto the hoof when domestic situations do not allow for natural hoof wear. The basis for some of this theory is the study of how mustang hooves wear in some specific western North American environments.

That precise kind of wear is often held up as a proper template to be emulated by the trimmer. This is from where the term "mustang trim" derives.

Farriers traditionally have provided all aspects of hoof care, both for horses with shoes and without. It is typically asserted in the barefoot movement that the trim that evolved in the mainstream, therefore, was one in which the hoof was trimmed with the idea of shoeing in mind. In other words, it is thought by farriers generally that a good trim must be put on a foot before it is shod, therefore, that pre-shoe trim is a correct trim. Specifically, in comparison to many of the new barefoot trims, heels are left longer, the hoof edge is rasped sharp, and the toe is left both longer and sharp.

In contrast, the alternative barefoot trims are most notable for a more petite look caused by taking more heel off, removing any flare from the sides, and providing the major noticeable difference, a "break-over" in the toe of the front feet. The break-over is where the front third of the hoof of the front feet, and rarely done in the hind feet, is angled or beveled, eliminating the sharp, long toe. This arrangement is said to provide a more natural pivot point in the step, so the flex and mechanics to the foot and leg structures are more natural and better for the horse. It also is generally explained in barefoot trimming literature that this trim should insure a heel first landing, placing the bulk of the weight landing onto the heel, which may not always be the case in a more farrier style trim where toe first landings are more likely to occur. Thus, horses with such a trim are thought to have a reduced risk of injury, an overall more proper balance of motion, and better performance.

"There's nothing wrong with a horse going barefoot," says Dr. Tracy A. Turner, DVM, MS, Diplomate ACVS, of Anoka Equine Veterinary Services, in Elk River, Minnesota. Dr. Turner's specialty is equine lameness, and his career includes stints at Colorado State University, Perdue University, University of Illinois, University of Florida, holding the position of Chief of Large Animal Surgery at the University of Minnesota, and he was inducted into the International Equine Veterinarians Hall of Fame in 2004. He also worked as a farrier before entering veterinary medicine and published the now somewhat classic article, "The Art and Frustration of Hoof Balance", in the *American Farrier's Journal*.

"I try to have all my competitive horses go barefoot some time of the year," he says of his Eventing horses. "If your horses don't need shoes, don't put shoes on them. I'd choose to have a horse go barefoot over being shod in general."

On the topic of barefoot trims, however, Dr. Turner has words of caution.

"Some are really radical," he explains. "My rules-of-thumb are: anything that draws blood can't be good. Anything that leaves your horse lame afterwards, can't be good."

This may sound obvious, but his professional advice comes from personal experience. He has witnessed instances where radical and bloody trims were performed on horses' feet by self-professed barefoot trimmers in the name of healing troubled hooves, which had sad and ultimately fatal consequences. He stresses, however, that a good trim is a good trim, regardless of who does it—farrier, trimmer, or horse owner.

"I support the idea of a break-over," he continues. "That rolling effect is probably correct. It is something we try to do with shoes, too. But, I don't know where that ideal point is. Horses are different, and some horses will be on either side of the average. Chincoteague Ponies in Virginia are not going to have the same foot wear as mustangs in Nevada. Don't make all horses conform to certain rules. When the rules become more important than the patient, then there is a real problem with the rules."

Dr. Turner had the opportunity to work with zebra populations in South Africa. Zebras from mountainous regions, he says, had different hoof wear and shape from those in lower plains regions, which points to the fact that an equine's environment has much to do with what is best for hoof shape. Such adaptations and allowances, he says, are not always made when humans assert the benefits of a kind of hoof trim based on relatively small herds of horses in a certain climate and environment, and then proceed to promote it as a singular answer, without scientific research, for all horses.

The American Farrier's Association, Dr. Turner explains, established a basic correct trim for shoeing, and it is the best ground-zero for a barefoot horse. He believes it is fine to deviate from that to some extent, particularly if a horse has individual needs, or if the season or environment might warrant it, as long as the horse is better for it and no radical alterations are made which lame the horse. He says to keep in mind, though, that more hoof wall also means more protection for the hoof; the more you cut away, the more open the hoof is to injury.

"The break-over can be from slight to high degrees," says Terrie Wood, a professional barefoot trimmer based in Riner, Virginia. "It's something you play with. I try to create a healthy foot with a healthy frog. One that is balanced for that particular foot. Sometimes I might even leave a sharp edge at the toe, if it's going to be wet, for better traction. I trim every horse differently, and the front are always different from the hind feet . . . and, a foot will change, too."

Wood has spent a decade educating herself, attending clinics with the most notable barefoot trimming experts, and trimming horses full time for a living. She is well respected in the area for her trimming and is in such demand she often has difficulty clearing a day off.

"I have learned from lots of different people," she says, "but I don't follow any one method. There is too much variation that you need to be able to use your own judgment on. I don't want to be thought of as limited to one type of barefoot trimming, and there is absolutely no difference in many of these trims really, anyway."

Certainly staying away from shoes is less time consuming, less expensive, avoids piercing the hooves with nails, and reduces some potential hazards during riding. Also, boot technology has advanced, making it very easy for the barefoot rider to simply slip boots onto the feet, if needed, in difficult terrain, such as jagged gravel.

"Barefoot is more forgiving than shod," Wood says of her experience. "A shoe can mask trouble sometimes that could show up later. If shoes are coming off, it takes a year to a year and a half for that foot to give you a true identity. Except for horses that do a sliding stop and have sliding shoes, those horses that are in rings . . . they could go barefoot."

As with many aspects of horse care, finding a capable farrier or trimmer, and getting the best hoof care for your horse at any given time, requires that a horse owner investigate matters. Clearly a growing number of people are trying out barefoot trims, and with that surge of interest also comes a growing number of people trying out the trade of barefoot trimming.

Whether or not these trims are all that different from each other, or a huge jump from the mainstream farrier's trim, is arguable and highly variable (not to mention, the regular farrier may already be the most knowledgeable "barefoot" type trimmer in town . . . you never know until you ask). Ultimately, it is up to horse owners to educate themselves as much as possible on the subject and ask around as to the quality of a particular farrier's or trimmer's work.

It seems most professionals across the board agree that keeping a horse barefoot is preferable if there is no real need for him to be shod. Short of that, as long as no harm is done to the horse, some experimenting may prove your horse does very well with a certain trim. If you are in tune with your horse, you will know soon enough.

CHAPTER 9

The Abernathy Boys ride in a parade in New York City to honor Teddy Roosevelt. *(Photographer: Paul Thompson [Illustrious Career and Heroic Deeds of Col. Roosevelt the Intellectual Giant, by Jay Henry Mowbray, copyright 1910 by Geo W. Bertron])*

THE ASTONISHING ADVENTURES OF THE ABERNATHY BOYS

This article originally ran in the April 2009 issue of Horse Connection Magazine (www.horseconnection.com).

This is a true story.

Bud and Temple Abernathy made three extremely long rides horseback unaccompanied by adults in the early 1900s, and were so young it is necessary to preface this article with, this is a true story.

Beginning in 1909 at the tender ages of five and eight, the boys made six journeys. Three were made by the brothers alone on horses. Each of the six was epic by any standards, and all were made within a four year period. Their accomplishments are factual and well documented. Their fame spread nationwide and grew so extensive they spent months at a time in the headlines of major and minor newspapers. The Abernathy boys were rock stars of their era, and household names to most Americans of that age—easily as recognizable at that time as Teddy Roosevelt and Buffalo Bill.

In the long history of long riders, these two hold a particularly special place in the ranks of the Long Riders' Guild (www.thelongridersguild.com). This international organization is comprised of equestrian explorers, all of whom have made continuous horseback journeys of 1,000 miles or more.

The acclaim for the Abernathy boys is held first for their achievements, which alone are extraordinary and unsurpassed even before their ages are considered. In fact, The LRG officially states that their third long equestrian journey was, "*The* North American-USA ride of the 20th century. No human being, man nor woman, has ever come close to doing what those tykes did on that ride."

These boys took their first long ride horseback during a summer break from school in the Oklahoma Territory in 1909 for something to do besides hanging around the family ranch. They talked their father (a marshal in the area and the only parent, their mother had died some time earlier) into allowing them to ride their horses, an Arab named Sam Bass and a Shetland Pony cross named Geronimo, 1,200 miles round trip from Frederick, Oklahoma up into New Mexico to Santa Fe and back. This they accomplished alone and had many incredible adventures including being chased while on their horses by a wild, crazed "jackass," enduring terrible weather, encountering a savage pack of wolves in the night, and coming across camps of Native Americans with whom they had trouble communicating. Despite the many obstacles they faced, their tenacity held firm and the journey proved a success. Rather than quench their thirst for adventure, however, as their father had hoped, it only made the boys thirsty for more.

The following summer after a great deal of diplomacy with their father, they were off once more. This time journeying all the way to New York City from Oklahoma horseback—again unaccompanied by adults. A film, *The Grand Ride of the Abernathy Boys* recently was released about this trip by the Independent Film Project of Oklahoma University (www.abernathyboysmovie.com). Their fame spread far and wide by this time, and an avalanche of newspaper stories were written about them as they progressed.

"Temple . . . invariably runs away whenever he sees a woman coming toward him," reported *The New York Times* on June 13, 1910, shortly after their arrival in New York City at the end of their second long ride. "The elevator proved his refuge last evening, and if any of the guests at the hotel paused to ask him a question even, he would make a quick exit to the elevator. 'I'm tired of folks asking me questions,' he said to a reporter with whom he struck up a friendly acquaintance, 'and I'm not going to let anybody take my picture any more. I want to be with my papa, and I want to have some fun.'"

Bud and Temple complained about people pestering them with "Kodaks," and they even enforced a "no kissing" rule to keep the crowds of zealous ladies at bay.

"Abernathy Boys put Ban on Kissing, Fearless Youngsters, Who Have Ridden Here from Oklahoma, Mobbed by Women," read the headline in *The New York Times* on June 12, 1910. It reported, "It seems that Temple has steadfastly refused to allow himself to be kissed by women ever since he set out on the long journey overland, and the only woman who succeeded in getting a kiss from him lives in Washington. But it was a bargain on the lad's part, for he sold the kiss for a quarter. . . . Louis [Bud] showed just as much embarrassment as his younger brother when several women insisted upon kissing him, and tried his best to escape, but finally had to submit, to the extreme disgust of Temple, who was now perched upon a chair near by."

As they approached the east coast, souvenir hunters stole Temple's Navajo saddle blanket and would rip out tail hairs from their horses.

Upon the boys' arrival in Washington, D.C. on May 28, 1910, a month before arriving in New York, *The New York Times* stated, "After riding on horseback most of the way across the continent to meet Col. Roosevelt on his arrival at New York, Louis and Temple Abernathy, aged 9 and 6 respectively, sons of Jack Abernathy of Oklahoma, the wolf catcher and friend of the former President, arrived here to-night. They rode in from Frederick, Md., to-day, a distance of fifty-seven miles. Temple dropped off to sleep the minute his head touched the pillow. While the little fellow was curled up restfully, Louis talked of their trip. 'Temple and I,' he said, 'want to see some of the animals Mr. Roosevelt sent from Africa, and to-morrow we will go over to the Smithsonian Institution to see if we can have a look at some of them.' When asked what he intended to say to Mr. Roosevelt when he met him in New York, Louis replied that it 'would depend on what Mr. Roosevelt said to them,' and that 'he could not cross that fence until he came to it.' President Taft will receive the little travelers. When the boys arrived in Washington they rode up and down Pennsylvania Avenue for some time looking for a 'wagon yard' where they might 'tie up' the horses. Not finding such a convenience in the National capital, they finally stopped at one of the best hotels and their horses were taken to a near-by livery. The boys will remain here several days."

Bud and Temple experienced no shortage of adventures on this trip included meeting Wilbur Wright and getting an offer to ride in his newfangled "aeroplane," being received at the White House in Washington, D.C. by President Taft himself, and finally meeting up with an old family friend they knew in New York City, Teddy Roosevelt. They rode their two traveling companions from this trip, Sam Bass and a red and white Pinto pony named Wiley Haynes, just behind the ex-president in a parade celebrating Roosevelt, down 5th Avenue with a million people lining the streets looking on.

With this 2,000 mile horseback journey now complete, Bud and Temple returned home on a different mode of transportation.

The boys bought a one cylinder used car called a Wildcat. After three hours of driving lessons, they headed out of New York and drove all the way back to Oklahoma.

Even with all the amazing adventures to this point, the Abernathy Boys' equestrian magnum opus would yet unfold in the summer of 1911. Now superstars across the country for their earlier feats, a challenge was put to them. Two businessmen agreed to pay them $10,000 if they could ride horses from New York to San Francisco in 60 days. The boys' father, Jack Abernathy, believed they could do it, and okayed them to go. Conditions of the wager stated they must only eat and sleep outside, and the boys agreed, but stated they would not ride on Sundays, sticking to their regular Christian day of rest even with the carrot of such a purse dangling before their eyes.

The day was August 11, 1911. Bud and Temple, now ages 11 and 7 respectively, and hardened from 3,200 miles in the saddle, set out from the Big Apple on their veteran mounts, Sam Bass and Wylie Haynes, for the west coast. The boys, now riding to cross the continent at a swiftness never before achieved, kept up a hectic pace of around 60 miles a day. This allowed for none of the sight seeing and fun of the other two trips, even though crowds of people came out to see them and many invitations for diversions were extended. The hectic pace made the third long ride a grueling undertaking that lacked the capricious encounters of the former.

Many extreme difficulties were overcome by the Abernathy Boys on this trip, the rule that they must only sleep outside certainly adding to the brutal nature of such a trip, but the lowest point of all their journeys occurred after leaving Cheyenne, Wyoming. There, Sam Bass got into a field of alfalfa, gorged himself, foundered and died. Even in the shadow of this heart wrenching setback, the young boys were determined to continue. They purchased another horse, Big Black, for Bud and set out again to finish the journey.

Wylie Haynes didn't take well to the newcomer. Losing Sam Bass put the boys behind schedule to achieve the goal of making San Francisco in just 60 days. Even with such brutal challenges as crossing the Great Salt Lake Basin in blistering heat to make the mountains on the far side and falling ill with food poisoning from a bad can of tomatoes, they closed in on their destination shattering all previous records.

In the Sierra Madres, they encountered sleet, slowing them yet again. Still, the resolute duo pressed through and then pushed hard for the coast. Bud and Temple Abernathy made the trans-continental ride in 62 days, missing the money by just 48 hours. Regardless, they said they didn't mind losing the bet because they knew they still had achieved an amazing feat. Curiously enough, the journey running in the opposite direction from San Francisco to New York just had been completed by "Two-Gun Nan" Aspinwall, the first woman to ride across the continent (www.thelongridersguild.com/2-gun-nan. htm). She arrived in New York in July 1911 having spent 180 days in the saddle.

The adventures of the first two rides were chronicled by family member Miles Abernathy. He spent some time fishing with the boys, and in 1910, penned the stories as they were recounted to him. This book, *Ride the Wind*, was long out of print, but a copy was discovered by the Long Riders' Guild, and they have re-published the work through their publishing arm, Horse Travel Books (www. horsetravelbooks.com). Also available are two other books written about these amazing little long riders: *Bud and Me* by Alma Abernathy, Temple's widow, and *The Remarkable Ride of the Abernathy Boys* by Robert B. Jackson.

CHAPTER 10

Martin Black in the A-Pen. *(Emily Kitching [www.eclectic-horseman.com])*

TRAINING INSIDE THE TRIANGLE
THE A-PEN WITH MARTIN BLACK

Martin Black is known to many through his books, articles, videos, and clinics. I've written several articles about Black's work over the years. This one stands out to me due to the innovative use of the unique corral it describes. It ran in the February 2007 issue of Western Horseman, and my original draft is provided here. A video on the A-Pen is available for ordering at Black's website, www.martinblack.net, along with his other videos, books, and a listing of his upcoming clinics and ranch schools.

Working a horse in a relatively small area defined by fencing has at least one big advantage: it provides the human access to a horse without the chance of the bigger, faster animal heading for the hills and avoiding lessons altogether—with or without the human aboard. Once acquainted with any type of corral, the shape and arrangement of the fencing can offer aid in a variety of ways. Anyone interested in horses is likely familiar with basic corral shapes including square, rectangular, oval, and (the recent superstar of pen shapes) round. The geometry of corrals may seem pretty well covered by this list, but wait . . . now there also is focus on the triangle. Martin Black, a fifth generation Idaho rancher and popular horsemanship clinician, has developed a triangular type of pen for the specific usage of starting horses on cattle, and adding what he calls "defense" to more experienced cow horses. Black refers to it as the "A-pen," and a few, built to his specifications, have begun to spring up on ranches.

Martin Black works a cow in the A-Pen.
(*Emily Kitching [www.eclectic-horseman.com]*)

Interest in Black's use of this A-pen is growing. His extensive cowboying resume is enough to turn heads and includes: a management position on a 1.25 million acre ranch running 400 horses and 15,000 head of cattle in Nevada, starting over 400 head of colts annually, earning over $50,000 in stock horse events and over $25,000 in the NRCHA. When asked how he sees himself fitting into the horse world, he replies, "I don't like limiting my vision to labels."

His business card has one, however. It reads, "Equine Empiricpsychoanalyst." What does it mean? Black laughs and explains, "It's a five-dollar title for a fifty-cent cowboy." Actually, it's a joke, but the irony is in its accuracy . . . look up the words and it essentially means, "one who works on a horse's mental and emotional well being in ways depending upon practical experience without relying on scientific principles."

A broad vision, vast experience, and openness to experimentation was clearly the key to developing his usage of the A-pen. "Bits and pieces fell together from cow work," Black says, and he is confident in this type of corral as an aid for getting horses better at cutting, rating, and working cattle. Several of Black's clinics now have been devoted to teaching his A-pen methods, and a video is currently in the works which will share this unique approach to starting horses on cattle, as well.

Australian Origins

The A-pen isn't exactly new, but it is rare to this country. Black spent quite a bit of time presenting clinics in Australia. There, he says he became familiar with the dominant cow-horse sport in that country: "camp drafting." This event is not organized under a central authority, like with cutting or reining in this country for instance, and there are no regulations regarding pen sizes or even exact shapes. Camp drafting has more of a local rodeo flare. People get together with whatever adequate facilities they might have available in their area to stage the event. Therefore, the size of the cut out yard for the sport vary widely, according to Black, but they are typically of the triangular variety.

"Camp drafting to Australians is what cutting is to Texans," Black declares. In this sport, he explains, about eight head of cattle are placed in the triangular shaped pen. A rider cuts one cow from the herd and pushes it out the gate into the arena and through a cloverleaf pattern around markers (he describes them as "pegs" in the ground); it is like barrel racing while driving a cut cow. "They start before dawn and go 'til after dark," Black says of the event's popularity in some regions.

The event is judged in two parts: work in the cut-out yard and running the course. The two separate scores are combined for a final score. In the cut-out yard, the herd-work phase is completed with the cow (or the "beast" as they say in Australia) being cut from the "mob," and pushed to the gate at the narrow end of the pen. If the rider loses control of the cow and it gets back to the herd twice, then he is disqualified.

In camp drafting events, nearly all the riders "go for broke," Black has observed. He thinks of cow work divided into two parts: offense and defense. Any time a horse is pushing the cow to move, it's offense, and any time the horse drops back and is blocking the cow from getting past him to return to the herd, it's defense. "It's like basketball," he offers as an example, where a player with the ball is like the cow trying to get back to the herd. That player makes an offensive charge with the ball towards the basket. Then the defensive player works to block him to keep him from the goal, like the horse and rider attempt to do with the cow. The typical rider in camp drafting, Black observed, just tries to push a cow through the pattern as quickly as possible, so the mentality is all offense. This tactic, however, often causes riders to lose control he says. Riders are scored on their controlled offense, but without a defensive turn in the cut out yard and the ability to rate back on the course when needed, they can be disqualified by the dreaded crack of the whip.

In Black's Australian clinics, he has begun to try to show folks how to build some defense into their cow horses. Not only does he feel this improves performance for the camp drafting enthusiasts by reducing the number of disqualifications from losing cows in the cutout yard, but he insists tracking and blocking a cow are essential skills for any working ranch horse as well. This work of sharing some cutting logic and ranch skills with these riders in the outback put him on the track to using the triangular type corrals in an innovative way. These pens were available to him at most of the clinics he conducted in Australia. As Black used them, he discovered their shape was well suited for working on defense and building a horse's confidence on cattle.

Setting Up an A-pen, Martin Black Style

Black has experimented with several A-pen sizes and settled on a layout that works best for him. The basic arrangement is essentially a triangle with its tip cut off. The triangle's bottom is a fence 100 feet wide. From either end of that base side, 120 feet long fences begin. These two run upwards evenly towards an apex, where they would meet at the tip as an isosceles triangle, except that Black then cuts the would-be tip off with a short twenty foot fence. This short fence chops off the point of the triangle and is parallel to the back fence at the bottom.

When using the A-pen, Black keeps a herd of cattle behind the fence at the bottom of the triangle. The holding pen is best arranged as an alley running the length of the 100 foot fence, split in the center by a partition. Gates should be in the back fence on either side of that central divider around the mid-section of it, allowing access to the A-pen from either pen behind the 100 foot back fence. With this configuration, fresh cattle can be kept to one side, easily brought into the pen and worked, then simply sent to the other side when done and thus automatically sorted, streamlining the process.

Using the A-pen to Start Horses on Cattle

With a single cow in the A-pen along with the horse and rider, and cattle in one or both pens behind the back fence, it is time to get started. One of the benefits to this set-up is that a single rider can work with training a horse to cut; no additional help of turn back riders and/or cattle dogs is required. "The herd creates a draw for the cow," Black explains. "The cow's goal is to get to that herd; your goal is to hold the cow off the back fence in the middle of the pen."

The physical layout of the A-pen builds in two critical factors that make it successful for Black's method. First, he employs the cattle's natural herding instincts in the pen's design. Simply by placing a group of her buddies behind the pen's back fence, a goal for the cow is created—to get back with them. By positioning your horse between that cow and the back fence, you have the perfect scenario for cutting. With this corral, however, unlike typical cutting where the herd is loose in the pen with the horse, if the cow gets by the horse, it can't return to the herd. Indeed, Black expects the cow to get past the horse. He provides this as a choice which will be an integral part of the horse's lesson, discussed a bit later. The object, according to Black, is to help the horse find the right positions to be in for improving its ability to cut. This is accomplished better with the A-pen scenario since the extra chaos created by a loose herd does not interfere with the clear understanding that is presented to the horse as relates to the one cut cow.

Second, aside from establishing the cow's goal simply by its layout, the A-pen's shape also provides the rider the ability to dial up or down the intensity of the cow's desire to get around the horse. As a horse pushes the cow up the A-pen, the distance from the herd increases, but also the two 120 foot sides begin to squeeze in closer together. This claustrophobic quality magnifies the cow's actions, and as a result, the triangular shape provides the rider quite a spectrum of offensive and defensive energy levels to choose from. This all can be accomplished by one rider from the back of a horse.

Once the physical understanding of how the A-pen works is established, Black then concentrates on explaining the horsemanship techniques he has found work in tandem with it. "If the cow isn't pushing on you," he says of the basics, "it means that you can step towards the cow, that you can be on offense."

"An important point the A-pen teaches a horse is to read where the balance point on a cow is," Black explains, "this is what actually affects the cow to move right or left. If we push towards the cow's tail, it will move one direction; if we push towards its nose, it will stop and turn the other direction. The point on the cow at which the response changes is the balance point. The balance point is not always consistent, it can change at any given moment. All we need to do is work the cow along the fence on foot and we will learn this real quick—when we get too far out of position, then we have to work harder to get back and get in control of the cow. This is what I want the horse to experience, to balance or hold the cow. When the horse balances or stops the cow, he is rewarded by a short rest. Out of position relates to work; position or balance relates to rest."

With Black, there isn't a constant bunch of tearing around the corral when working to get a horse to cut. Most often calm steps are the norm after the horse has learned where position is. Pressure and release is employed on the horse to give the horse a chance to figure things out. Black works at making the right thing easy for horses in the A-pen, so they begin to want to cut in good position. He works from the premise that the horse naturally can do everything he is looking for already, like rate, stop, and turn. Then, if he makes it a little more work for the horse to be lazy about a job like rating the cow, or keeping in good position for cutting, it won't be long before the horse figures out to do it right, because it is just simply easier for him that way.

"I want the horse to travel in a straight line from the turn to the stop, whenever possible," Black says, for example. "Any wandering out of the stop I allow is just allowing the horse to get in trouble." But Black allows the horse to get out of position, so that he can learn it isn't the best way to go. If the horse essentially figures it out for himself, then he will gladly work that way. And why not? It was his choice. On the other hand, if a person fights with the horse to try and impose his decision on the horse's movements, even if it would be the best choice as relates to the situation with cow work, Black thinks the horse probably won't understand what is being presented, and at the very least could be resentful about it.

"You'll see me letting the horse wander out," he continues, "but I'm offering a defensive turn. If he's not listening to me, fine, but he's going to create more work for himself wandering out there.

At some point, even if I'm clear up to the point [of the A-pen], that's going to cause the cow to push back on me and make him go all the way to the back fence [by the herd]. I'm going to hustle him back so it's more work for him to get back and then let it be comfortable for them to be between the cow and the back-fence. Then I will give them a lot of time to think, this makes them cautious about coming out, because they don't want to have to go to work hustling to get back."

"Horses pick this up really fast," he continues. "It's confusing for a lot of people because it contradicts a lot of things we're used to hearing in relation to cow work. I don't worry about keeping my horses flat, I don't worry about stopping straight, I'm aware if they are or if they're not. If they're not, I'm creating more work for them, so basically they teach themselves that it is better for them to stop straight, or better for them to collect themselves and come through a turn."

When a horse is in a good position, you may see Black letting the horse just stand for several minutes. This easy time for the horse is his reward for being in the right position, and to the bystander unaccustomed to the practice, it may seem like Black is doing absolutely nothing much of the time. It is these opportunities to do nothing that allow the horse time to soak in the lesson and to feel good about being between the cut cow and the herd. "When they get their heart rate up," Black says, "I like to get their heart rate back down." Often he uses small steps to put the horse on the offense, getting equally small responses from the cow, with plenty of nothing in between.

On the other hand, if the cow comes towards the horse, Black wants the horse to switch to defense. "I don't like to mix the two," he says. "In other words, if the cow's got me on defense, and then she turns to go to offense, I'd like my horse to stop without going towards the cow. Just stop and turn—make a defensive turn. Like a basketball player on defense. You're not trying to push her, you're just making a defensive turn." If the cow gets by, then he scrambles the horse back to the fence and gets between the cow and the back fence again to start over. The overall scheme of efficient cutting will then just naturally unfold to the horse.

Black's innovation with the A-pen can get a horse tuned up, often in a few sessions. Typically, horses starting out won't understand exactly what is being asked of them, he explains, but then, quite suddenly the A-pen lesson can click and they get it. At that point, there can be a big change in horses and their cutting skills can fall into place. The adaptation of the camp drafting pen to this unique usage follows from, as Black says, "Growing up on a ranch short-handed, trying to do the work of several men yourself." If you are starting horses on cattle, whether or not you find yourself short handed, the A-pen might be a sound investment to consider.

CHAPTER 11

Stoney, well after his initial introduction to our farm. *(Carol Moates)*

NEW HORSE HEALTH AND SAFETY

This story of Carol's horse, Stoney, arriving at our place with some unwanted guests ran in both Equus and The American Quarter Horse Journal in different versions.

Handfuls of stringy spaghetti-like white worms, little curly cue red worms, and red acorn-sized things that looked like strange drill bits that might be used to bore through hardened steel littered the ground. Some still squiggled in the manure that had exited the leopard Appaloosa gelding overnight since his arrival at our farm the day before. It felt like stepping into the set of a science fiction/horror film with creepy alien creatures everywhere—and believe me, I wanted them beamed out of here.

In actuality these intestinal parasites were alien creatures to our farm. The regular de-worming schedule here produced a long standing safe and parasite controlled environment for our herd. I flipped out at the distressing sight that lay before me and immediately called trusted vet, Dr. Kim Gemeinhardt, DVM, owner of Latitude 36 Mobile Veterinary Services in Germanton, North Carolina for advise. She helped us get through our immediate dilemma. She also provided insight into many other potential medical problems that can hitch a ride in with a new horse and how to stave off such medical misfortunes. It is a real situation co-mingled with sound veterinary advice that many horse owners may find valuable.

Stoney was a spur of the moment purchase for my wife, Carol. He fit her riding needs perfectly, was a handsome dapper gentleman covered from head to toe in black spots, and his former owner (the friend of a friend) sadly had become disabled by MS and needed to move him quickly to a new home. The gelding already had been moved from the owner's place to her father's farm when we first inspected him. At least a dozen other horses were around, and the answers to all our basic questions regarding worming, vaccines, and general health care seemed satisfactory. The fellow appeared to be a knowledgeable, honest, and handy horseman. The gelding was in good flesh, proved alert, had an appetite, and showed plenty of energy. No coughs, nasal discharges, or any other outward signs of illness were detectable. It was a short trip between farms and the owner's father offered to deliver the horse, so we agreed.

It was just dumb luck we had a corral at a corner of the farm completely isolated from our other horses where we put the newcomer at first. At the time Stoney arrived, five other horses lived on the farm. It was December, and we just recently had administered a round of the broad spectrum de-wormer, Equimax, to these horses. The post-freeze, heavyweight de-worming is an annual event on our farm to help control nearly all regular parasites as well as tape worms. The rest of the year we administer either ivermectin or pyrantel pamoate, alternating years.

Even though the fellow who negotiated our purchase of the horse indicated to us that his daughter kept Stoney up to date on his de-worming, I figured it was unlikely he had been given the broad spectrum de-wormer that we had just provided to our horses. So, the minute Stoney stepped off the trailer I gave him a dose to be in sync with the others and put him in the isolated pen until we could see the next day what new herd arrangements might best be suitable.

Stoney's winter coat was a bit course and lackluster. We didn't think much of that since every horse we've ever brought home improved in appearance with daily hands-on care, decent feed, and proper access to the equine mineral supplements. The next morning when I went out to feed was the shocking moment when it became evident that the new horse had not been de-wormed on a regular schedule, nor in recent history—and I wondered from the looks of things if he had ever been de-wormed.

Now we were faced with two problems: treating a horse with serious and multiple parasite infections, and, as Gemeinhardt dutifully explained, taking careful measures to avoid our other horses becoming infected.

It is a lesson, we've discovered from numerous conversations since then, that many other horse folk also learned through painful experience. A friend with a boarding and training facility for example, where many horses come and go frequently, shared multiple instances of such trouble caused by new boarders coming in with parasite infested mounts.

It was very lucky Stoney was isolated from the moment he stepped onto the farm, so at least all the passed parasites dropped on the ground in one contained area hundreds of feet from any other paddocks. I took stock of what I could see and described these to Gemeinhardt.

Most obvious, and what easily caught my eye at first, were white worms. There were tons of them in the manure, many still moving, and of varying lengths up to about two inches long. These were ascarids. Then there were the very strange reddish, spiral looking creatures with one sharp end and the other one blunt, some an inch long, which were bot larvae. Tiny white bot eggs had been attached to the hair on the gelding's legs when he arrived and we had scraped them off with a bot knife already. Finally, it took a close inspection of the manure to see little, spiral, thin, red worms. These were thread worms.

Gemeinhardt's first caution was to remove all the manure from the isolation corral either off the farm or completely away from other animals to another isolated spot. She stressed that these parasites transfer readily to the other horses if allowed to come into contact with them. There are plenty of far off corners to our property, so we carefully picked up all the gelding's manure and carried it to a lonely place. The task became more difficult the second day when the manure turned quite watery and even larger loads of the parasites passed. It was necessary to shovel some of the dirt out with the manure to get it all at that stage. I wore rubber boots for the task and cleaned them well before traveling to other areas of the farm.

To ensure a solid kill of all parasites, Gemeinhardt suggested a second round of the broad spectrum de-wormer be given six days after the initial one to kill any newly hatched out parasites or any that may have survived the first round of de-wormer. We followed her protocol and took the advice of maintaining an additional five days of quarantine after that follow-up dose, again with the manure carefully removed to an area safely cut off from all horse access.

Our example shows some initial good luck followed quickly with implementing sound veterinary advice. The result was that our herd's health was maintained, and Stoney was brought up to proper condition and introduced to the others safely. It was a great lesson which, along with the additional advice from Gemeinhardt, provides an effective protocol to prevent some basic health threats from arriving at your farm with incoming horses. Parasites, however, as

Gemeinhardt soon explained, are not the only kind of trouble that can fly in under the radar with an infected horse and contaminate a previously tranquil equestrian paradise.

"There are a number of concerns when bringing in a new horse," says Gemeinhardt. "Diseases are not always apparent; there can be in-apparent carriers, and they can really mess things up quickly."

When looking at a new horse, a pre-purchase veterinary exam is a good first line of defense against bringing equine health problems to your home, Gemeinhardt explains.

"A pre-purchase exam is just a kind of wellness check," she says. "Many people are doing this now to try to make sure they are not transporting disease. I explain to people that there are things that can be hidden in these horses that by listening to their lungs and looking in their eyes, we're not going to be able to tell. If I'm doing a pre-purchase here for a horse to move out of state somewhere, I will often want to contact a local veterinarian where the horse is going to see if there are any certain diseases going on in that area that I should vaccinate this horse for before it travels, so that we have immunity upon arrival. We have a lot of really good vaccines out there and we just need to know to use them. For example, if you're shipping a horse from one area of the country where there's no influenza, and your going to an influenza epidemic area, you certainly want to vaccinate for it."

The pre-purchase exam can be made more effective, Gemeinhardt says, if blood work is done in addition to the physical exam. This is particularly advisable for higher risk horses.

"If a horse is coming through a sale barn, or a boarding barn, where there's lots of activity and horses are in and out," she explains, "running a blood panel on them before they are shipped is not a terrible idea. It is not something that everybody thinks about, but many times it can show us underlying concerns that we cannot see by doing a physical exam. I will suggest this routinely on my pre-purchase exams, although not everybody takes advantage of it.

"A low grade infection or a compromise of one of the metabolic functions—liver, kidney, this kind of thing—may be evident. There are many enzymes and elements that are measured in a chemistry panel, but really what is of great interest to me are the blood cell counts because it can indicate, for example, if the horse is anemic, perhaps it's highly parasitized, or if there's a high white cell count, perhaps it is coming into or getting out of having some type of infection. It is relatively inexpensive compared to bringing a sick horse into your barn, and they can be done very rapidly. Most places can get the blood test back in one working day—if you're going to send a Coggins in on a horse you're going to transport, and that takes a couple of days, you may as well do a panel with a blood cell count so that you have that information as well."

The next line of defense against contamination to a farm from a newcomer is to quarantine the new horse. Stoney's inadvertent isolation saved us a good deal of trouble by avoiding the spread of parasites to the other horses, helped us to see the parasites easily in the first place, and shows the value of making the measure a customary practice for incoming horses. Gemeinhardt points out that isolating a horse in no way harms him and can save a tremendous amount of difficulty should parasites or infectious disease be transported with him and makes the job of detecting health issues much easier.

"A minimum of 10 days, but I would feel more comfortable with three weeks," Gemeinhardt suggests regarding adequate quarantine time length. "If they pick something up in transport many times it does not become apparent for ten to twelve days. Watch for general signs of disease: coughing, runny nose, depression . . . anything that shows something might be cooking. That feeling you experience when you're 'coming down' with something—horses get that same feeling. Horses can even pick something up in a trailer. Stuff happens really quick sometimes."

"If an isolated horse starts to show swelling from strangles," she says as an example, "you might not think much of that swelling if it is in a herd—horses knock into each other. If the horse is in isolation though, there is no excuse for that kind of thing. It is more clearly evident. And isolation doesn't mean across the fence where they can still touch noses. It means NO contact. Get as big a distance as is physically possible. Isolation is the trick. It is so important. Plus, if they break with disease, you can deal with the contamination in a smaller area."

Strangles in particular is a disease Gemeinhardt uses to illustrate the tricky nature of detecting disease. "The horse can be shedding strangles, Streptococcus equi, for all of its life and yet not show signs of disease, but can infect everybody else. Sometimes if you are going to be bringing horses in, it's better to update your horses at home as well, other than just worrying about the one that's being transported. It would be very specific from region to region, or even barn to barn. It is certainly much less expensive to try to prevent disease than it is to treat it."

Our experience with Stoney makes Gemeinhardt's advice a cornerstone of operations around here. With so much invested in keeping our horses healthy, a few extra steps at the critical moment of transporting a new horse is a small nuisance in that big picture. The horrifying moment of discovering those parasites piled around in that corral is forever branded in my memory. I leave you with Gemeinhardt's sage advice that can save you and your herd from ever enduring that nightmare:

"If I have the luxury of a couple of days, I will really push to de-worm the horses where they are coming from. Let them leave those parasite there, and bring them to your property as clean as possible. I like to de-worm three days before they transport, that way if I'm upsetting anything in the digestive system I've got time to clear it up before they get on that trailer."

CHAPTER 12

EVELYN CAMERON: THE COWGIRL PIONEER OF PIONEER PHOTOGRAPHY

Evelyn Cameron is simply one of the most interesting women in western history. The extensive journals she kept daily for many years, along with the large body of photographs she made at a time when photography was still in its infancy, is an astounding historical record. I wrote this article largely from a personal desire to work up a profile of this incredible woman. Eventually, I. M. Cowgirl magazine was lined up to publish it, but the publication went under before the feature ran. I'm pleased to finally gain it an audience by including it in this collection as a previously unpublished article.

It is likely the rarest glimpse of life on the American frontier through the eyes of a woman ever to exist, both in terms of written memoir and photography.

The survival and subsequent discovery of Evelyn Cameron's diaries, papers, and photographs may be just dumb luck . . . or perhaps divine intervention. Whatever the cause for the good fortune, these remnants from a bygone era on the Great Plains at the dawning of the 20th century are a singular treasure.

They are also clearly the by-product of Cameron's own extraordinary life story and personal tenacity. This unlikely Cowgirl Hall-of-Famer (inducted in 2001) began life in 1868 on a sprawling estate to a privileged family, an ocean and half a continent away in England.

A rough and rustic ranch near Terry, Montana at the closing of the 1800s, however, proved to be her soul's true home. In this world where little time or resources existed for capturing the happenings of daily life, this innovative and resourceful cowgirl worked overtime to do just that. The results are bestowed on us today as an avalanche of outstanding time-capsuled information. Cameron made time for daily diary entries, often by lamp light after long, brutal days hacking out a living on the raw land in the elements . . . and not just a smattering of autobiographical details, but a complete set of 35 years of daily journal entries (1893-1928) complete with all kinds of side notes in the margins regarding every tiny aspect of her life, from eggs sold to calves lost.

As a self-taught photographer with a bulky and burdensome mail order 5x7 Greyflex camera, at the dawn of photography itself, Cameron shot for posterity a most amazing collection of images of life in the wilds and frontier settlements of Montana. To provide badly needed income, the tenacious woman packed the colossal camera and tripod on her saddle horse, sometimes for days, all over the countryside going to photograph customers where they lived. The resulting collection of more than 1800 photographic plates and 2500 printed photographs depicting people, livestock, wild animals, rough country, and fledgling towns is extremely unique. There are even self-portraits, often of Cameron at the manual tasks about the ranch like milking a cow or standing on the back of a horse she trained herself, telling much of her own lifestyle.

And therein lies one of the great statements Cameron made by how she lived her adult life. She was born, Evelyn Jephson Flower, into wealth on an estate south of London. Her half brother, Cyril Flower, in juxtaposition, became Lord Battersea in 1892. She could have remained in a life with groomed Thoroughbreds saddled by servants and never a thought given to how the cream arrived to her tea cup. Certainly her family and friends pressured her to come to her senses. Instead, she chose the cowgirl trail less traveled by her kind—one of hard physical work and very rustic accommodations in the wilds of North America.

Perhaps the first tell-tale step of Cameron's independence from the shackles of gentry, certainly a sign of determination to follow her inner compass regardless of outer influences, was in her marriage to Ewen Cameron. Ewen came from the Scottish aristocratic class, but his family was penniless by comparison to the Flowers. He was a rugged, outdoorsy sort and spent much time out in the country studying his life's passion: birds.

Their honeymoon first brought the couple to Montana in 1889. A former cavalry scout for Lt. Col. George Custer guided them through the badlands, and they fell in love with the place. A year later they bought the land near Terry and moved in. Their overarching business plan was to raise polo ponies to transport back to England for sale. That particular venture was a complete disaster several difficult years in the making, but the tough, close to the wilderness lifestyle there invigorated the couple in many ways. By the turn of the century, they gave up the polo pony breeding idea and were small-scale ranching on the prairie, trying to make a go of it.

In Ewen, Cameron had a renowned ornithologist husband whose head often remained more in the clouds with the birds than on practical matters on the homestead. The couple took in borders. Evelyn received an annual allowance from her family and was able to produce more income than the average cowboy in that area by selling produce, eggs, and other goods off the ranch. Ewen published articles in various British scientific magazines and was a skilled hunter.

To this eclectic mix of livelihood, Evelyn soon added photography. Her work in this new field generated income, but also images of incredible aspects of the west rarely glimpsed in our age. She captured common people on the frontier, even the very poor and often outcast immigrants, in their own environments. As a trusted member of the sparsely scattered population of that region (one-of-them in the truest sense) she seemed able to elicit a reality and honesty for her camera not always found in photos from the time. These photographs, along with all of the Camerons' papers including Evelyn's diaries, were boxed up and hidden from the world for more than half a century.

Happenstance seems a far-fetched explanation for the discovery of this life's work. Especially since it happened to be a Time-Life Books editor, Donna Lucey, who in the late 1970's discovered the collection stashed away in the basement of a property owned by the late cowgirl's best friend—Cameron left everything including the ranch to Janet Williams. Lucey instantly grasped the significance of the find, quite literally masterpieces by the dozens, providing an incredible insight into the lives of early settlers in and around Terry, Montana.

Thanks to Lucey, the extraordinary Cameron is nowadays widely known, and her work highly regarded. After years of sorting the photographs and studying Cameron's diaries, Lucy published *Photographing Montana 1894-1928: The Life and Work of Evelyn Cameron* (Mountain Press), a photo-book that beautifully depicts Cameron's photographic genius and her unique personality. Another book, *Evelyn Cameron: Montana's Frontier Photographer*, by Kristi Hager (Farcountry Press), was released in 2007.

She is rightly, as mentioned earlier, in the Cowgirl Hall of Fame, and PBS recently produced a two hour documentary on this remarkable woman, *Evelyn Cameron: Pictures from a Worthy Life*. The film's title was taken from Cameron's own words written shortly after beginning her life in Montana, "I wish I would lead a life worthy to look back upon. I am far out of the path now."

Cameron's diary from 1899 is available in its entirety in digital form on the Internet, offered as part of the Montana Memory Project for the public to read (http://cdm103401.cdmhost.com/u?/p267301coll2,1293).

Second Lady, Lynne V. Cheney, showed her admiration for Cameron when addressing an audience at the National Cowgirl Museum and Hall of Fame in Fort Worth, Texas in 2001. She greeted the attendees and went straight to talking about Evelyn Cameron, using her as a preferred example to describe the cowgirl spirit she embodied:

> *They [Ewen and Evelyn Cameron] came hoping to build a fortune by running horses and cattle on the prairie, but as in so many stories of westward migration, they didn't find that pot of gold. Evelyn found*

something else, though, a life that appealed to her immensely. There were no social classes as there had been in England. Instead there was a spirit of equality. There were no pretenses. Instead there was hard, invigorating work. Evelyn wrote to a niece in England, "Manual labour . . . is all I care about, and, after all, is what will really make a strong woman. I like to break colts, brand calves, cut down trees, ride and work in a garden."

Hard work, she firmly believed, was the cure for sadness, the remedy for heartache. When a young friend's letter to her indicated a perilous emotional state, Evelyn Cameron invited her to come visit. "I have so many stock chores to do that I do not feel in a position to entertain a guest," she wrote, "but I know you won't mind that and you can help me pitch hay, feed chickens, etc. These are the tonics that will make you feel the world is not such a bad place after all."

Coming from, and rejecting, a privileged English background, it seems Cameron thought of the people back in that world as her audience at times. Clearly, Cameron valued the hands-on dirty work kind of life, which was in direct contrast to the upstairs/ unsoiled exploits of the privileged class she knew as a young woman in England. Many of the self-portraits that depict her working at various manual tasks around the ranch were sent to her nieces back in England to expose them to the life she led and valued as worthy.

Perhaps, what spurred her on to record so much of her life was the hope that other young privileged girls like she had been would come to understand that they, too, were not bound by British social conventions. That being born into the aristocracy did not have to be their destiny—that life could be an adventure full of creativity and possibilities lived on one's own terms.

Ewen died in 1915. Evelyn, however, did not waver from her chosen path. She continued on, running the ranch until her own death 13 years later.

CHAPTER 13

Jay and Kyle Shaw move in to usher a bronc out of the area at the Miles City Bucking Horse Sale. *(Allen Russell [www.allenrussellphoto.com])*

TOUGH ENOUGH:
MILES CITY PICK UP MEN

One of my favorite aspects of the rough-stock rodeo events is watching the pick up men do their job. These horsemen put in a lot of hard hours and while guaranteed a paycheck, like stagehands in a successful stage production, they often seem less noticed and celebrated by the audience than the riders. I enjoy speaking about them in articles whenever I get the chance. Photographer, Allen Russell (www.allenrusselphoto.com), lined up the opportunity for me to interview

*the pick up men featured in this story which ran in the January/February 2011
issue of America's Horse magazine (www.AQHA.com).*

———————————

Clang! The chute swings open. The bronc bolts into the
arena surrounded by packed grand stands and breaks into a hard
buck. In a second, the cowboy loses his grip, goes over the hind
end, gets catapulted, and seems to hang there airborne. The bronc
charges forward at a wild gallop even before the cowboy has time to
land face first in the dust. The horse hardly gets two strides before
being surrounded by three riders in matching blue shirts galloping
along with him. One leans over and deftly snatches the bronc rein.
The horse is efficiently ushered out of the arena. The pick up men
reposition. The next chute opens . . . .

The scene sounds like a rodeo, and it is one of sorts, but this
is not your typical bucking horse event.

"It's a lot more work than just a rodeo where you have a
bunch of old horses that's been bucked," Kyle Shaw says. Since
1997, he and his son, Jay, have been pick up men at an unusual
bucking horse event held each year: the Miles City Bucking Horse
Sale in Miles City, Montana (www.buckinghorsesale.com).

The unique Miles City Bucking Horse Sale just celebrated
its 60th anniversary in 2010. It is held the third full weekend in May.
Horses consigned to the sale are showcased in action during the
bucking horse event. Many rodeo rough-stock contractors are on
hand looking to add fresh horses to their bucking strings, and the
livestock in this event come from all kinds of backgrounds.

"The old horses that's been in the bucking string for awhile
[in typical rodeos]," Kyle continues, "they know that their job is done
when you show up, and they pretty much know you're going to help
them out to get the guy off. At the bucking horse sale, some of the
hardest horses to pick up are old saddle horses, 'cause they're not
afraid of you. You can't hardly push them—they'll cut behind you,
turn around and go the other way, and they're just a lot harder to get
close to."

Both of the Shaws are Montana ranchers. Kyle, who is 53, lives thirty miles south of Miles City and has his own place. Jay, 31, manages a ranch nearby with 4,000 head of mother cows owned by former astronaut, Frank Borman (who was Commander of the 1968 Apollo 8 mission and one of the first three men to circle the moon).

Two pick up men are usually used in rodeo events, but the large numbers of inexperienced bucking horses coming quickly through the chutes at the Miles City sale event make an additional pick up man necessary. It takes three, each with his own string of seasoned and capable horses, to manage the mayhem and stay on top of things to be ready for every out. For many years now the third member of the team has been another Montana rancher and American Quarter Horse breeder, Lynn Ashley (www.ashleyquarterhorses.com).

"I think going to the bucking horse sale compared to a rodeo," Jay says of the pick up work, "it could be overwhelming. You have a lot of horses that you see through the course of a day, and you don't know any of them. So you have to really be on your toes to read what's going on. It's a lot more outs. It takes a lot more horses. I'll end up hauling seven or eight horses into that deal to stay mounted good enough, so I've always got something fresh enough to get the job done, compared to a rodeo where you might haul four or five horses."

It isn't difficult to get on the topic of what makes a great pick up horse with either of the Shaws. Both have ridden primarily registered American Quarter Horses on the ranches and for picking up in their careers.

"They've got to have a lot of heart and not be scared," Kyle says. "Although I used to think you want a fairly aggressive horse, but several of the better pick up horses I have had over the years were probably the most timid horses in the bunch when they were turned loose. But they, for whatever reason, decided when a person was riding them, that they could be the aggressor and made really good pick up horses. They've got to be willing to take a lot more punishment as far as being kicked and banged around than just a ranch horse. You can take a real good ranch horse, get him kicked and stuff like that, and he'll say, 'The heck with you!' We need the one that says, 'Okay, bring it on!'

"They have to be an athlete and have quite a little speed and agility to do the job because it's a hundred miles an hour, then you change directions and go the other way. Then they have to have an awful good mind because running horses is hard on a lot of horses' minds—they get all excited. Running next to another horse, the competition comes out in them. The Quarter Horses are athletic as far as the stop and turn and quick starts. The bigger boned, bigger footed horses I like way more than the smaller type of horse. The height . . . keeps you from getting kicked in the knees as much."

Jay agrees that a sound mind is a critical asset for a first-class pick up horse. It is especially true when working the Bucking Horse Sale, since the bucking stock there, when compared to that of rodeos, is uncommonly inexperienced to the environment and all over the place in the arena.

"In my string of horses," Jay says, "they all have plenty of speed, but you can get by with a slow horse if you can keep his mind settled down. They've got to be broke to ride. There's none of this gee hawing, kicking them around type of deal. And if their mind can't handle it . . . pretty soon they just won't stand it. They'll run, then you can't get next to your bucking horse. You can't get next to your cowboy to save him. I've got several that Lynn Ashley and his brother have raised. Lynn, he strove to ride a bigger horse that would handle going to the hills and roping steers and stuff like that, and when he started picking up, I'd been riding some of his horses by then, and it's been a good deal for me. They've got a good program and I've got a place to go get them. We use them on the ranch all the time and go ahead and take them to the rodeo on the weekends. They earn their keep every day."

Jay is partial to the Ashley Quarter Horses', Zan Parr Bar bloodline. Three of his current string are from this line and he says they are some of the best American Quarter Horses he has ever ridden and his favorite pick up horses ever. Again, it is the mind of these horses that most impress him when picking up or at home.

"They kinda crave it [picking up]," Jay says, "but at the same token their mind is like a rock. You can take them out there, drop the reins over the saddle horn, and watch a bucking horse go and he doesn't do anything till I tell him. One horse is just a five year old I started this year. And the other horse is ten years old but, I bring him home. I've got two girls [Cady Jo and Paige]—one's five and one's three—and they jump on him and ride around the countryside. I'm really impressed with the line, the mindset on them, that they can take that much pressure and act like that. Zan Te General, that's the one horse I really am kind of sold on. I've had several guys try to buy that horse, but with the girls being at home and learning how to ride, I'm not going to sell him because, heck, he takes too good a care of them."

The other horse Jay really likes is Zan Te Levi.

"The General horse, he's about 16:1 and probably weighs about 1400 pounds," Jay explains. "He's a big horse. The Levi horse is about 15:2, probably weighs 1300, just stocky, heavy muscled, short top line. They're both roan horses, ones a blue roan, the other's a bay roan. The girls call them Kip and Kap."

Jay Shaw and his young daughter who already seems to have the makings of a cowgirl. (*Allen Russell [www.allenrussellphoto.com]*)

These two horses in particular, Jay says, are completely consistent and dependable day in and day out, and neither one of them has got a mean bone in his body. It is reassuring to him that his girls can safely be riding or petting on these two gentle horses. In fact, Jay says he has seen Kip and Kap stand firm and protect the girls when they were in a corral with other horses and the herd went to milling about.

Ashley Quarter Horses is a family run outfit that has specialized in breeding performance and ranch horses for four decades in southeastern Montana. Aside from striving for excellent conformation, the Ashleys pride themselves on breeding horses with "quiet dispositions and trainable minds." They raise cattle commercially, as well, so the horses they bring along are no strangers to a working ranch environment.

"He [Lynn] enjoys what he's doing and it shows in the horses that they're raising," Jay says.

For the Shaws, not every ranch horse makes a pick up horse, but every pick up horse has to be a working ranch horse.

"I've never had a horse that had a single job, like [just] being a pick up horse," Kyle explains. "They have to work cows, sort cows, and pick up and everything to be here because of the expense of keeping them for one thing. It's really a trial and error thing. You get one, and then you get to playing out in the pasture loping along and pushing each other around, bumping each other, and if they don't like it, they're not going to work. It's a lot like kids and sports; if they like it they're a lot more aggressive, if they don't, they aren't."

The Bucking Horse Sale clearly puts pick up horses to the test. These days the number of bucking horses accepted in the event is limited, but that wasn't always the case.

"Dad and I picked up 500 in three days [one year]," Jay says. "It was nuts and we were sore, our horses were sore. Then after that they started putting a cap on it. The way that it's changed around now is that they've got the match bronc ride on Sunday; they bring in all the top guys and the NFR horses. That day is pretty easy. In the course of the weekend this last year we picked up a hundred and fifty some horses."

Kyle has decided to retire from picking up the bucking horse sale. 2010, he says, was his final year. As far as jobs go, there surely are less dangerous and physically demanding ways to earn money.

"It's one of the few jobs in rodeo that you can go take your horse and get a paycheck every time you go—as opposed to competing," Kyle chuckles. "A guy wouldn't do it if it wasn't fun, I don't think. The paycheck isn't what keeps bringing you back. You get to know a lot of people so it's like a weekend out with the guys, and you get away from your other concerns."

"If you're doing it for the money, you're doing it for the wrong reason anyway," Jay says. "It's not a get rich deal, by no means . . . . If you don't crave a little adrenalin, and if you're not willing to take a little bump and bruise here and there and keep on going, it's really not the job for you. If you don't have a little but of grit, you probably better not do it."

CHAPTER 14

Linda Hasselstrom on the ranch in South Dakota.
(Jerry Ellerman [2011])

"WOMEN OF THE WEST:"
LINDA M. HASSELSTROM

After spending a winter reading quite a few books that Linda Hasselstrom wrote or co-edited, it occurred to me with her ranching background in South Dakota she'd be a perfect fit for Western Horseman's "Women of the West" department. The editors agreed, and I was extremely pleased she was open to an interview. The column is presented as a collage of quotes without narration other than a short introduction. The July 2010 issue of Western Horseman included her interview. The original draft was shortened to fit the magazine's space requirements; here the full text of the original draft is provided with previously unpublished quotes.

Recently, Hasselstrom won the 2010 WILLA award for creative non-fiction from Women Writing the West for her new book, No Place Like Home. She continues to give writing retreats at her prairie home in South Dakota. "Most of my retreats consist of me and from one to three women discussing and revising their writing," she explains. More information is available at: www.windbreakhouse.com.

Linda M. Hasselstrom is a renowned non-fiction writer, poet, and editor. Family ranching in the shadow of the Black Hills of South Dakota is the foundation of the life she has known since the age of nine. The body of literature she has worked to create since the 1960s speaks directly and deeply to her experience as a rancher. Her books have received many awards including a Wrangler Award from the National Cowboy and Western Heritage Museum. Currently she lives at Windbreak House on her ranch where she writes, conducts writing retreats, cooks constantly, and remains immersed in the land she loves—the source of her inspiration. (www.windbreakhouse.com).

Once I moved to the ranch, I was still an only child, and if I didn't entertain myself, my folks found something for me to do—like hoe the garden. Working with cows taught me that if I observed their actions, I could anticipate what they might do. So I learned that animals are not inanimate things, but intelligent beings who share our world. A horse was the ultimate: not only a warm friend, but a real companion who responded to my actions and what I said to her in ways that made it clear she understood and respected me. If I treated her badly, she'd let me know I shouldn't do that; she taught me to be embarrassed about behaving badly. And the nicer I was to her, the more she trusted me and performed her work with joy. I will never stop missing that horse or the others I raised and trained.

The rural westerners I know are not very vocal, particularly about physical or emotional pain. They grew up understanding that success requires work, and that equality of treatment is based on equality of effort. Folks from other places may see westerners as stoic or unfeeling, because their passion for their land and their families isn't something they reveal lightly. They buckle down to hardship, but they take time to notice the meadowlarks singing.

I think ranchers must learn patience to succeed, and animals are capable of teaching the hard way if one isn't a willing learner. I suppose I shouldn't assume everyone is capable of identifying with animals, but I hope it's true. When I got my second horse, Rebel, she was wild and unbroken. We came as close to being one organism as is possible; I rode her bareback with reins loose, guiding her by leaning. I'll never lose the feeling of that closeness, and though I like dogs, cats, and cows, I've never felt it with any other animal than a horse.

We don't dare "get used to" death; our job is preserving life—for the range, for the cows, for ourselves, all in balanced harmony. I don't know how I would have responded to the deaths in my life without that upbringing, but I have found joy in living despite those losses, and I remember the people I've lost often and with appreciation for their lives. I do believe my early experiences with birth and death helped me accept life more fully and live it more wisely.

The West is changing, but I don't believe its essence will disappear. Our history is only a couple of hundred years old, but because it's all we know, we fear and resist change as all humans do. We've used that time to learn about the land and we know now that to plow grassland is to destroy an association more ancient and precious than any agricultural experiment might devise. If we want healthy grasslands —for cattle, bison, open space, clean air, pure water—we need to keep the ecology intact, including the predators. Ranchettes promoted by greedy ignorance are degrading some fine range land, but they won't fill it all. Ranchers are learning how to speak coherently about their good stewardship, how to cooperate with lovers of wildlife and wild space to protect what's important to all of us.

Both terrain and weather have always been important in creating real westerners because they demand so much from us, and I think they always will be. Some of the ranchette people, like the first homesteaders, will move back to town, or try to turn the country into a town that coddles them. Others will learn how to love the country responsibly on its own terms and thus become "real" westerners.

Twenty years ago, I saw a herd of about thirty cows being moved by ten shiny new pickups and said to myself, "That's what's wrong with ranching."

Machines require gasoline a rancher can't produce, and they can't do everything. As our economy adjusts to new world situations, and people start concentrating on saving the landscape as well as saving money, many will discover that horses can be used for many jobs more efficiently and cheaply than gas-eating trucks or even four-wheelers. And if things get really tough, you can't eat a pickup.

My father, intent on making me a worthwhile human, bought a cow for me to milk. I moved cattle on foot until my uncle gave me a horse, and then my dad wouldn't let me use a saddle until I had mastered getting back on after a mishap. One of my aunts, who had her own horses, her own brand, her own checking account, showed me how to be a strong woman while insisting she was not a feminist. I grew up thinking I could live happily all my life on a South Dakota ranch—but my father insisted I go to college. Westerners live comfortably with these sorts of contradictions.

By the time I got back to South Dakota, I was convinced that responsible ranching was important to the health of the Great Plains. My life elsewhere had demonstrated to me that many well-meaning folks who care about "the environment" can't understand what healthy land is and what it requires of its residents—because they've never had the opportunity to work on the land. Meanwhile, people who work on the land may be too busy to explain their work or hostile because they are afraid of change from the outside.

Since I'd straddled several possible lives, I thought I might be able to help bridge some of the gaps between people who work the land and those who don't. When I began writing about the ranch, my work was often rejected, but in 1987 my diary of a year on the ranch was published by a very small (one-woman), independent press, and reviewed favorably in *The New York Times*. That event focused my attention on what has become my life's work: writing about grasslands and its inhabitants. At that time, "rancher" and "environmentalist" were considered to be incompatible roles, and the idea that a person of intelligence and education might choose to do physical labor was anathema to most educators.

I've often said that a month on a ranch, especially during calving season, could prevent teen pregnancies and exposes one to every conceivable aspect of life and most of the moral dilemmas. Calving causes everyone stress, but we all talk to the animals as we work with them, hoping to reassure them of our good intentions.

Quoting *Windbreak*, "One could say this is simply because the cattle are more valuable if they are healthy, but that's not all of it. All of us talk encouragingly to a heifer when we are pulling her calf. The talk isn't practical because even the sound of our voices is not necessarily calming to her. It is simply a kind of communication, a desire to let her know that we'll stop hurting her as soon as we can."

Much as I resist generalizations, I have to say that women definitely hold western families together. Sometimes the men are a little too busy polishing the myth or maybe simply too busy keeping the ranch solvent. Men make or buy the signs that say "Jones Family Ranch," but women take the pictures, write the letters, keep track of the community history by remembering who fathered that child and often by reminding him of his responsibilities. (The inexperienced may call this gossip, but as Meridel LeSueur often remarked, what women remember is the history of the tribe.) Lately, more and more western women are finding their voices, either by holding office, speaking, or writing about their lives, so that a truer picture of the reality is finally emerging.

CHAPTER 15

Allen Russell and his Quarter Horse, Kono, at the edge
of Mirror Lake in the Colorado Rocky Mountains.
(Allen Russell [www.allenrussellphoto.com])

FROM SEA TO SHINING SEA
SEEING SPACIOUS SKIES AND PURPLE MOUNTAINS MAJESTIES FROM THE BACK OF A HORSE

America's Horse, the American Quarter Horse Association membership magazine (www.aqha.com), ran this story in the October 2008 issue. It documents two rides made across the United States in the mid-1970s. One was made by John Egenes and Gizmo from the Pacific to the Atlantic and the other by Allen Russell and Kono from Canada to Mexico.

Allen Russell's ride is particularly notable because he took a back country route through the Rocky Mountains for most of the trip. Russell is a remarkable photographer, a professional with decades of experience, and assignments have taken him to every continent but Antarctica. Many of his photos have accompanied my articles in recent years. His website, www.allenrussellphoto.com, documents "Life in the American West" and has been profiled in the photography magazine, Shutterbug.

John Egenes is an American, but in recent years has moved to Dunedin, New Zealand. There he completed a masters degree in music and now lectures at the University of Otago. He also enjoys notoriety as an Americana songwriter

Allen Russell and Kono stop to rest and search for water
at an abandoned sheep camp in the Red Desert of Wyoming.
(Allen Russell [www.allenrussellphoto.com])

and multi-instrumentalist. Several CDs of his music have been produced, and more information about him is available at www.johnegenes.com

---

North to South Allen Russell and Kono

"I truly wanted that experience of wandering," Allen Russell says.

He wasn't kidding. Russell and his American Quarter Horse, Kono (King Hoppy Kono) wandered alright . . . all the way from the Canadian border down along the Rocky Mountains through the entire length of the United States to Mexico. 2,400 miles of wandering, to be exact.

"I felt I was born in the wrong time," he continues. "It used to be people were able to just wander horseback. I wanted to get a feel for what that feels like . . . get to know the country I live in a step at a time. I had total confidence that if I started in Canada and kept Kono's nose going south, I'd hit Mexico. It worked, even though I often didn't know where I was."

Russell and Kono's cross country trip may not be one of the longest rides ever recorded, but they stand out for another reason. The trip they made from the northern to southern borders of the United States was done almost completely along back country routes.

"The primary difference in my ride and most others," Russell explains, "is that I rode totally back country, not along side roads or an established route. From Canada to Mexico, Kono and I rode along roads maybe 50 miles total. Much of the time we bushwhacked and even established trails often didn't lead where we wanted to travel."

1975 was the year they made their trip, long before hand held GPS devices, cell phones, or even the first laptop computer, so getting lost was a lot easier then. Still, Russell says that given the choice today, he would leave the gadgets at home.

"To me, that just ruins the whole thing," he says of taking electronics into the wild. "It seems to me the point of doing it is to get away from all that. On my trip, if I had broken a leg up on a mountain somewhere, I would have died . . . it adds a lot to the sense of accomplishment. You have to pay attention. It's the real thing. Today we live in a world where there's always safety nets."

Russell chose the extremely challenging Rocky Mountain route not just to get away from modern conveniences (even those of that time) but also quite simply to avoid fences. He lived on a little ranch in Oklahoma and had done some day work on quite a few others, as well as taken a few rides around the lands out west, so he was well aware of how the countryside was criss-crossed with fencing. Riding miles in one direction looking for a gate, or laying fences down and then repairing them over and over did not appeal to him, or ranchers either for that matter. Neither did sticking to existing roads the whole time. So, when he looked at a map of the country with this trip in mind, the Rocky Mountains with their naturally difficult geography that often passed through the vast open lands of National Forests were the obvious route for him.

"There's a real art to waking up in the morning, looking at a mountain range, reading it, and getting through it without having a dead end and having to double back," Russell explains.

To get started, Russell and Kono were trailered up a road to the west of Glacier National Park. They rode to the Canadian border and then into Glacier to start their trek southward.

"I was an experienced horseman," Russell reflects on that moment, "but I wasn't an expert mountain traveler."

The first four weeks of the trip proved to be the wettest Montana spring in 30 years. It rained all but two days in the first month on the trail. Kono was sore at first, and Russell had to be extremely careful with him as they made their way. It was cold and wet, and in the first week they reached the Flathead River, which was swollen with the water from the recent rains.

"I sat looking at that thing for half a day," Russell remembers. "I eventually built up enough nerve to jump in. It was a quarter mile wide. Water jerked me off that horse. Kono went across pretty good. He was standing there eating when I got back up to him after hiking back upstream from where I ended up."

The lesson from that day, Russell says, was to dismount and stay on the downstream side of the horse when crossing deep rivers.

Of all the many challenges and achievements on this journey, if you ask Russell what stands out in his mind the most, his answer is direct:

"In my opinion, the greatest accomplishment of my ride is that I made it with one horse. It says an awful lot for him. And that's over really rugged terrain and two deserts—Wyoming's Red Desert and New Mexico's Journado del Muerte. When I realized 'Journado del Muerte', translated to 'Journey of Death,' I skirted around the edge of it."

For Russell, there was never any question what type of horse he would use for such a journey, either.

"I just always had been a Quarter Horse guy," he says. "The versatility has sold me on them. They have work ethic bred into them. I always have had registered Quarter Horses because I believe in breeding. I'm a student of bloodlines, a little bit, and there are sure traits that pass on.

"A good mountain horse is like a distance runner. [Kono] had the right conformation and I paid attention to that. Not really big . . . very well proportioned: 15 hands, nice neck, not real bulky. Kono was a bay with four black legs and hooves. After that trip I rode him a million miles leading pack strings around here; he never took a sore step in his life."

Russell knew he and Kono would have to stay on track to make the journey down the Rockies in one season. He started right at the end of the winter weather for Glacier, and he was aware that the northern mountains of New Mexico are known for their early snows.

"I thought we could make the trip in three months," he chuckles, "it took five."

Some long riders travel with one or more pack horses. Russell felt making the trip on a single Quarter Horse was the way to go.

"If you don't put your horse first, you probably won't succeed," he explains his one horse philosophy for the long ride. "If you have three horses, only one has to go lame to shut you down. Only one has to act up to greatly slow you down. I'll take one good horse any day and give him the attention and consideration he deserves in order to keep us going. The reason I went with a single horse is because the more horses you take, the more you set yourself up for failure. I wanted to be fast and mobile."

Aside from more potential for disaster with extra horses, there is simply more upkeep as well. Russell managed to do a little "cowboy shoeing" when necessary on the single horse. At night Kono was hobbled and accessorized with a bell, which was a simple means to keep the horse close, while allowing him to forage a bit.

"When I got to the border, people had found out, so when I got there I did a ceremonial ride over and back," Russell remembers. His parents were among those meeting him there. They trailered Kono and him back home.

"I wouldn't trade that experience for anything in the world," Russell says. "I'm a real believer in adventures."

West to East John Egenes and Gizmo

A year earlier, in 1974, another registered American Quarter Horse was ridden coast to coast: this one west to east from Ventura, California to Virginia Beach, Virginia. John Egenes had recently finished a three year tour in the United States Navy serving mostly on a submarine during the Vietnam War era. After that experience, wanderlust and the desire for wide open spaces attracted him to experience the country horseback.

"Originally I thought about Canada to Mexico," he says, "but I thought that wasn't really long enough."

Such ambition prompted him to mail to a Denver geological survey office for quality, detailed maps of the whole country. He studied these and mapped a general cross country course to take along a southerly route.

Escaping the confines of a submarine and military service may have helped jump start the desire to get horseback and head out across America, Egenes says in retrospect. But the seed for the trip was planted in his mind almost a decade earlier. Like many folks who later embarked on long horseback rides, the book Tschiffley's Ride, an autobiographical account of Aimè Tschiffley's 10,000 mile journey horseback from Buenos Aires, Argentina to Washington, D.C. in 1925, planted the seed for such a trip in his imagination as a young man.

"I checked it out of the high school library," Egenes admits, "and never gave it back. That [book] was the pivotal thing for me. That's what really sparked it."

Egenes grew up with horses, so a saddle was a familiar place for him. His family raised and owned American Quarter Horses in South Pasadena, California. At the time this trip was coming together, he had recently acquired and broke Gizmo, a Leo bred gelding from the family's stock. Gizmo, whose registered name was The Wayward Note, was out of a mare his mother owned that was a King Ranch horse, My Wayward Lady, and his sire was an excellent racehorse of the time, Palleo's Note. The four year old just happened to be in the right place at the right time to be chosen to make the trip.

John Egenes and his Quarter Horse, Gizmo, on the road.
(John Egenes [www.johnegenes.com])

"If I was going to look for a horse," Egenes says, "my first choice would have been a Quarter Horse."

"The horse is very much a part of the intrigue of a trip like this," he says. "You're disconnected . . . you're out there alone with your horse. When you live with a horse day and night, you get very, very close to them. Pretty much all the time out there, I'm just talking to Gizmo. The biggest thing is that you have to be comfortable just sitting around for hours."

Egenes spent quite a bit of time tracking down old U. S. Cavalry manuals and studying what information they had for making grueling long rides. The tips he picked up from them he stuck to religiously, and he believes helped to keep Gizmo's back from soring and the horse fit and healthy even in the more extreme conditions they encountered. These guidelines included getting off and walking the horse for 10-15 minutes every hour, not traveling more that 20 miles in a day, and giving the horse one day off each week.

"Some days we covered 20 miles in three or four hours," he says. "Then it is a temptation to go on. But, I just wouldn't. We made 120 to 130 miles a week. It is very difficult . . . you have to slow down. It is a very different mind set."

For gear, Egenes used a Canadian Mounty's saddle and some original McClellan U. S. Cavalry Army surplus saddle bags he found for $10 at a tack shop. There was food and a few tools in the saddle bags, otherwise, all he carried was a small day pack, a rain poncho, and a Colt revolver. He even cut the handle off his toothbrush and rode with only a halter to lessen the burden of weight on Gizmo.

Egenes and Gizmo set out from Ventura, California on April third. The first leg of the trip took them through California, Nevada, Arizona, and New Mexico. That made one of the first tests for the team crossing the Mohave Desert.

"I followed old roads or went cross country," he explains of traveling through that region. "There were no fences, I just followed the geological survey maps, but there was a time I got lost. Usually I always knew where I was because of those maps. It was very complicated out there. The first third of the ride was spent finding water every day. [Gizmo] lost a lot of weight; there wasn't a lot to eat.

John Egenes and Gizmo on the road in South Boston,
Virginia on the home stretch to the Atlantic Ocean.
(John Egenes [www.johnegenes.com])

It was tough till we got to Texas and Oklahoma."

Around the fourth of July, Egenes and Gizmo reached
Amarillo, Texas. They stopped by the AQHA headquarters while
in town, for a warm welcome and some picture taking. Then it was
back on the trail through Oklahoma, Missouri, Tennessee, North
Carolina, and Virginia.

Egenes says that one of the biggest points to understand
about a horse on a long trip is that they will lose some weight no
matter how much they are fed, particularly on the back at first. This
can cause a saddle which is a correct match to the horse at the onset
of the trip to lose its fit in a week or two. Great care must be taken
to watch for this and any other problems that might cause a sore.

"I was very much aware what was happening with my horse's
back," Egenes remembers. "By the time he was done, he was hard as
a rock!"

Fall was setting in as Egenes and Gizmo made the Blue Ridge
Parkway in Virginia. The towering, centuries old hardwoods with

John Egenes and Gizmo in the Atlantic Ocean at Virginia Beach, Virginia as they complete their continental crossing. *(John Egenes [www.johnegenes.com])*

their dazzling display of colorful autumn leaves were a stark contrast to the desert southwest they had set out into that spring. By the end, Egenes was ready to be done.

"Gizmo and I were in the papers everyday," he says about arriving in the east, "but all I wanted to do was finish the ride. And Gizmo . . . as soon as someone would say, 'Hey, how you doing?' he would stop. He became trained to it."

On November first, Egenes and Gizmo reached the Atlantic Ocean at Virginia Beach, the point he had chosen simply by looking at a map when planning the trip. In seven months they covered 4,400 miles on their long ride.

"The first time Gizmo balked at anything on the whole trip," Egenes says, laughing, "was at the ocean that day. It was like he was thinking, 'You want me to cross that? But I can't see the other side!'"

It took a little coaxing, but he finally got the gelding into the surf, and the coast-to-coast trip was officially finished. But now, pretty much penniless and on the opposite side of the continent from home with his horse, Egenes was faced with a new challenge—how to get back.

This is a part of the story where the AQHA plays a central role. It just so happened that Egenes ran into some Quarter Horse owners near the beach, and they invited him to stay at their place. After living on baled peanut vines and steady traveling for the last few days, Gizmo was pleased with the arrangement. These folks, as it happened, were just preparing to go to the AQHA Congress later that month in Louisville, Kentucky. They had an extra space in their trailer, and he and Gizmo were able to catch a ride at least back that far.

At the World Quarter Horse Congress, Egenes and Gizmo were guests of honor—the AQHA well acquainted with their endeavor from the pit stop they made in Amarillo. Again, AQHA serendipity was at play, and he met a horse trainer from San Bernardino, California who had an extra slot in his trailer and welcomed the extra driver along on the haul back.

Afterword

After returning home, Gizmo's reward for such a phenomenal performance was a year of turnout in a grassy pasture with a herd of horses. Gizmo went on several pack trips over the years. Egenes moved, with Gizmo in tow, to New Mexico. Gizmo lived a healthy life until 1992, when he had to be put down for health reasons related to aging.

As for Allen Russell and Kono, Russell says, "Kono continued on for many years as my main mountain horse in my Outfitting business in Montana. He was an amazing horse and never once let me down." Kono went to Oklahoma to spend his later years of life leisurely at pasture. He died in 1994 of old age.

CHAPTER 16

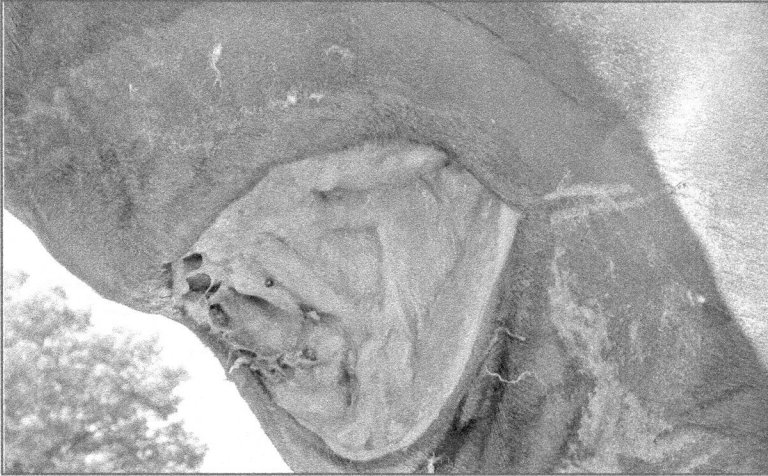

One side of Impression's horrible neck injuries. *(Dr. Kim Gemeinhardt)*

NEGATIVE PRESSURE WOUND THERAPY
FOR EQUINES

The first article I wrote on Dr. Kim Gemeinhardt's pioneering use of negative pressure wound therapy (NPWT) on equines ran in Equus magazine many years ago. Subsequent articles on the subject provided updates along the way and ran in The American Quarter Horse Journal, Horse Talk (a regional magazine in Virginia and Maryland), and Hoofbeats (in Australia).

NPWT is readily available since it has been widely used on humans for many years. The staggering results it has shown in the equine cases where Gemeinhardt has innovated its use keeps me hoping veterinarians will become more aware of it as a cost effective and quick wound healing option. The most recent version of the article appears here. It is an amazing story and I include it in this book hoping that it helps build awareness of the availability of NPWT to treat horses and other large animals.

A revolutionary use of a wound healing technology, called "negative pressure wound therapy" (NPWT), has been successfully adapted to equine veterinary use by Dr. Kim Gemeinhardt, owner of Latitude 36 Mobile Veterinary Services in Germanton, North Carolina. Gemeinhardt is licensed to practice in Virginia and North Carolina, and her innovative use of NPWT in equines has been reported in publications across the United States and as far away as Australia.

Gemeinhardt was introduced to the technology, which has been used in humans for nearly two decades, when visiting her father at nearby Wake Forest Baptist Hospital and was fascinated by a device being used to help him heal from a bed sore. Dr. Joe Molnar, from the Department of Plastic and Reconstructive Surgery of the Wake Forrest University School of Medicine in Winston-Salem, NC, was treating him using a NPWT treatment technique.

Gemeinhardt immediately saw potential for the therapy on the large animals she cared for. She approached Molnar about trying the NPWT system on large animals and was met with surprising enthusiasm. The plastic surgeon even offered to work with her in the field to help get the technology working for veterinary applications.

"I could tell Kim was very practical," Molnar explains of their first encounters. "We both saw the opportunity this could have for animals and seized it. I told her if she had a suitable patient, we could try this thing out."

Oddly, with the treatment being straightforward, relatively inexpensive, and widely accepted in humans with a decade of proven performance in hospitals around the world, its animal applications were limited to some initial testing on swine. When Gemeinhardt and Molnar connected, the right personalities clicked in place to change that.

Molnar jokes, "We'd used it on enough people to make sure it's safe for horses."

Horses with gaping wounds lacking tissue enough to stitch closed have had but a single option for treatment over the years, what veterinarians call "benign neglect," or "second intention," essentially leaving the wound to heal itself. Other than administering antibiotics and hosing out the injured area to keep it clean, little else could be done to facilitate healing such wounds. The chance meeting between Gemeinhardt and Molnar in 2000 changed that, adding NPWT to the equine veterinarian's nearly empty wound therapy tool box. NPWT allows for additional technical support to be added to the horse's healing mechanisms.

The NPWT

It wasn't long before a horse provided the opportunity to see just how effective NPWT might be in this application, running into a gate latch and tearing a gaping hole in its neck. Dr. Molnar generously shared NPWT knowledge gleaned from his human patients (along with some of the necessary equipment from the hospital) and worked hands-on with the equine project in the barn.

"Dr. Molnar is amazing," Gemeinhardt recalls. "He came out, and I even remember him on a ladder in the middle of the stall at midnight working."

NPWT uses a small electric vacuum pump to keep continual suction on a healing wound. A tube runs from the pump and enters the wound area through a plastic sheeting bandage covering the wound and sealing around its edges so a vacuum is created underneath. A sponge-like material is cut to fit the wound and provides air space between the drape and healing tissue to keep the bandage from collapsing. The tubing is embedded in this spongy area where it sucks out the dead cells and serum produced by the healing process. A flask in-line collects all the material that is wicked away.

This first attempt to use NPWT on a horse provided many challenges. "We put our heads together," Molnar says, "and that with a little duct tape got us going."

"That first case was a success in that we learned how to keep the VAC [as the NPWT is sometimes called] in place," Gemeinhardt admits. "We were unsuccessful at keeping the VAC on the wound for more than a couple of hours at a time."

Because of the learning curve in adapting NPWT to horses, the results pertaining to the healing time of that first horse likely did not show substantial improvements over the horse's natural healing ability. However, on that one case the team worked out all the major problems for applying the NPWT to horses.

"Healing times are at least twice as fast," Gemeinhardt says about using NPWT on numerous cases since, "but it's been even better than that several times."

Some of her early results were published in 2005 in the veterinary medical journal, *Equine Veterinary Education*. That information derived from the case of Impression.

Impression's Impressive Story: The Second NPWT Applied in Equine History:

As gaping wounds go, Impression's is as impressive as it gets.

"The guy who called is a real cowboy," Dr. Gemeinhardt explains, "nothing bothers him . . . his voice was shaking on the phone. 'Kim, can you come right now? This horse has a hole in his neck big enough to put my fist in!' That was the smaller wound. I could put my head in the big one!"

The nine year old gelding was found in a wooded pasture by his owner, Tracey Clayton.

"I went down where he was standing . . . with his head down," she remembers. "I saw the small wound first. When I saw the other side of that horse, I was not prepared . . . I don't see how he was still standing."

Impression had suffered two enormous wounds to the neck. The larger on the left side was more than eight inches by seven inches and over three inches deep, and the one on the right a little over half that size. Even early on, the wounds could not be closed; the deficit of tissue was just too great.

The first day, depilatory cream was applied to remove hair around the edges of the wound and a regular dressing was applied. The second day, Gemeinhardt uncovered the wounds and removed all dead or compromised tissue. With the information gleaned from the first case, getting the NPWT going on Impression was straightforward. Medical grade open cell polyurethane ether foam was trimmed to fill the wounds' cavities. Into these spongy hollows the evacuation tube was set. A single tube ran embedded through the foam in both wounds in series since they were so close.

With the foam and tube in place, the tissue adhesive Mastisol was applied to the depilated skin around the injuries and the wounds covered with a single adhesive drape and pressed firmly against the skin to set it and create an airtight seal around the perimeters of both wounds. The entire border of the dressing was then duct taped to the surrounding hair.

The evacuation tube with a liter flask in-line ran up and was attached to the pump mounted in the rafters to create the vacuum. An electrical cord was run well overhead providing power for the pump.

For further system security, the tube was anchored to Impression's mane and a stretch fabric neck covering provided extra strain relief. Finally, a wooden cradle modified with gauze and duct tape for cushioning was put around the entire area to limit flexing of the neck.

Treatment Course

Every three to four days, Gemeinhardt replaced the dressings and evaluated the wounds. She measured the dimensions of both at these times and created a table to document Impression's progress with the NPWT treatment. Her findings were that the wound quickly decreased in size from day two until day 12. The rate of reduction slowed thereafter until removal of the NPWT system on day 29.

The wounds decreased in depth as granulation tissue filled the cavities. As the wounds leveled out towards the end of the therapy, the foam dressings were reduced in size and the aspiration

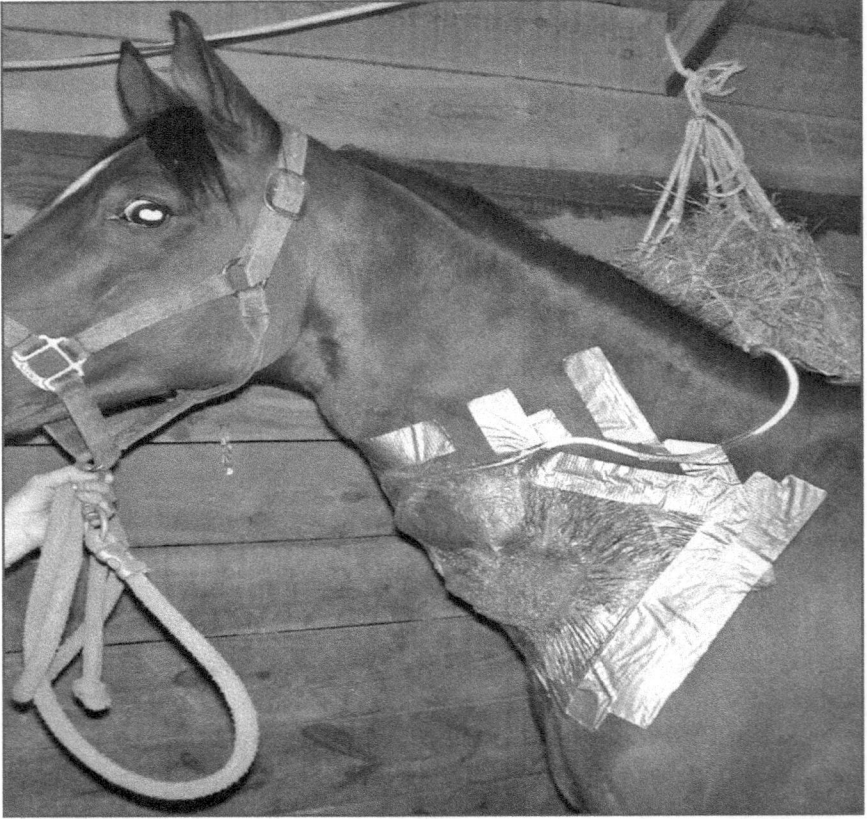

The NPWT device in place covering Impression's wounds.
(Dr. Kim Gemeinhardt))

fluid likewise steadily decreased. In the onset of treatment the flask required emptying every 10 to 12 hours, and by the completion of the treatment, the flask did not fill even after 48 hours.

Impression was kept in a stall during the 29 day recovery period. Beginning on day eight, some light physical therapy began by allowing short durations of in hand grazing. From day 14 on, the owner began to encourage the horse to gently extend his neck by offering carrots. This was employed to hopefully limit contracture of damaged muscles in the neck as they healed. Once the VAC was removed on day 29, the horse began light exercise being ridden.

Follow up care only required wet-to-dry dressings, with the wounds being flushed with saline solution at each dressing change. The stretch fabric hood also was kept over the neck until skin growth over the affected areas was complete and strong. Within the week after the NPWT was removed, the wound areas became level with the surrounding neck muscle. The final results proved fantastic with the horse retaining full mobility of the neck and the cosmetic results very good as well. The NPWT treatment in no way seemed to adversely affect the jugular vein, esophagus, or trachea even though they had been exposed to the interior of the wounds and, therefore, the pressure from the vacuum pump during the early phases of the treatment.

The results of Impression's case are particularly impressive due to the massive nature of the wounds he suffered. Even if the method of "benign neglect" had ultimately produced the same healing results and infection had not set in, the time needed for such a recovery would have been counted in months and certainly would not have been so far along in as few as 29 days.

Gemeinhardt sites the main reason for this success as the system's ability to provide overall cleanliness. The NPWT system tightly seals out any contaminants, but this alone doesn't stop infection. Rather it is the tightly sealed wound covering coupled with continual vacuuming away of any foreign matter from the wound cavity that is key. There never is the presence of bacteria in the wound space. This environment where everything but healthy tissue and blood supply is wicked away is the ultimate healing environment for a wound, keeping only clean, fresh blood supply along the healing surfaces and in the granulation tissue.

"I firmly believe the VAC system saved Impression's life," Clayton readily admits. She has ridden him at least three days a week since recovery without problem. The only remnants from the injuries are a slight indentation in one area of the scar and the memories of the trauma. In the winter months with a heavy coat Clayton says the scarred areas are completely undetectable.

The Future

The horses in this and several other equally successful cases since have tolerated the NPWT extremely well. Gemeinhardt explains part of the reason . . . "This is a non-painful bandaging system." It is known from human patients that there is no itching or discomfort caused by the vacuum in wound areas, so the horses haven't been inclined to rub or bite at them. Other than gentle nosing of the coil tubing from simple curiosity and some flexing of it from a horse's regular stall movements, the coil tubing was easily kept out of the way by taking it from the horse up and into the rafters above the stall.

Portable vacuum pump units are in the process of being developed. Placing these onto the horse or its blanket in some manner would make the NPWT system self-contained aboard the horse and allow a more normal horse lifestyle during recovery

In a matter of weeks Impression shows remarkable healing results.
(Dr. Kim Gemeinhardt))

periods, including a quicker return to exercise, than the present pump models which require shore power.

"I am continuing to research and refine the equine application of Negative Pressure Wound Therapy," Gemeinhardt says. "I am constantly modifying the technique. I have got it now to where I can do a dressing change by myself with a cooperative horse."

Another great benefit of NPWT is its cost effectiveness. The procedure is straightforward. The pumps are reusable. The tubing is cheap. The dressings can get expensive, particularly for larger wounds. However, any costs created by NPWT may be offset by the rapid healing times seen in these cases, thus requiring far fewer overall days of care, and can get a working horse back on the job much sooner.

Gemeinhardt, however, points out another extremely important benefit to this mode of wound care; once in place, she does not need to administer antibiotics. In this day of anti-biotic resistant bacteria, NPWT provides an extremely promising alternative to those drugs, thus helping to prolong their usefulness in this world.

Another perk, she explains, is that the NPWT dressing typically goes at least 48 hours without requiring a change. This reduces the wound's exposure to outside contaminants and decreases the work involved in caring for the wound.

Gemeinhardt hopes that her success with this revolutionary wound healing technology spurs interest in other veterinarians to realize the potential for NPWT in horses, both for recovery from injuries and to facilitate the healing of difficult surgical sites. With basic materials and pumps already available around the world for human applications, she explains, the jump to equine usage is mostly one of technique. Ready to share all she has learned, Gemeinhardt aspires to spread the word about her work and increase awareness of this option to help horses.

"As far as where we go next," Gemeinhardt offers, "I think it is a method that can be adapted to so many cases that its use should be considered by anyone dealing with wounds or difficult surgical sites."

CHAPTER 17

Escaramuzas charras in action. *(Jim Jennings/AQHA)*

ESCARAMUZAS CHARRAS!

The colorful teams of women that dazzle crowds with their precision horsemanship in Mexican rodeo was a fun subject to explore. This feature was written for a magazine that folded before it was able to get into print, so it is previously unpublished.

A rawhide reata sings and sizzles, slipping around a wide saddle horn, producing a plume of smoke that engulfs a mounted *charro* and gently slows a roped mare. A brass band plays from a grandstand off in the distance. The landscape is dotted with the big round brimmed sombreros shading the participants from the afternoon sun as the *charros* display their incredible roping skills in the *lienzo* (a keyhole shaped arena). Then . . . the rumble of hoof beats and a splash of color pours into the round end of the *lienzo*. The crowd bursts into roars and applause—it's the *escaramuzas charras*!

This is *charrería Mexicana*, the traditional Mexican rodeo. *Escaramuzas charras* are the horse women who ride and compete in the drill team competition which is part of the rodeo. The *charrería* is, however, much more than a competition; it is an equestrian folk tradition with cultural roots running deep in Mexican history. It is an extremely formal affair, and the *charras* (horse women) provide a sense of pageantry, color, and feminine splendor to the largely masculine Mexican style rodeo competitions, with their numerous *charro* (men's) events like bull riding, fancy roping, and bronc riding.

In beautiful flowing skirts, big smiles, and seemingly effortless sidesaddle seats the best charras create a sense of ease in their equitation. But don't be fooled, their performances are anything but easy. The complicated, synchronized drills performed by teams of *escaramuzas charras*, sometimes up to a dozen at once, are routinely extremely difficult. Their performances require tremendous athleticism and the highest degree of horsemanship skills. Regard to careful timing in the drills is of the utmost importance, and appreciation for this risk is not lost on the judges who grant more points for more difficult and dangerous maneuvers. The intricate weaves of patterns performed at high speeds during *escaramuza* routines are likely as difficult and dangerous as riding in any performance horse sport.

The roles of both women and men in *charrería* are fixed in established customs and held to exacting standards of horsemanship, tack, and dress. Strict rules in the *charro* federations of Mexico and the United States police the appearance of the contestants and their horses as much as their performance. Mexico's rich history is a major influence on these colorful and amazing equestrian folk traditions, and there seems little in this equestrian world without tangible historical references.

Only in the past few years have occasional cash prizes begun to be part of Mexican rodeo, and traditionally only the titles with their prospective trophies were presented to winners. The acclaim from such titles alone carry incredible prestige. The events are largely family affairs tied to Mexico's own identity, and the *charrería* has remained largely true to its roots even into the modern era.

"The majority [of girls] start off at seven or eight years old," says Carmen Quiñones, who lives in California and is the *escaramuzas'* Coordinator at National Level for the Unites States. "In my family . . . it's a sport we can all be involved in—travel together, be together, and we come home from school or from work and we're focused on one thing, our horses. I met my husband in this, and my boys are strongly involved. My oldest is competing in Guadalajara [Mexico] today with his team. And my daughter is ten years old so she is already starting."

Escaramuzas charras performing intricate drill team patterns.
(Jim Jennings/AQHA)

"It comes to be like a second family," Quiñones explains of the *escaramuzas* teams, "because we're always together. An additional girl that we bring is like an additional family that we adopt."

Escaramuzas charras add fabulous color, stylishness, and magnificence to *charreria*. These horse women compete in three events, the *punta* (a single run with a sliding stop), the *cala* (a reining competition), and the dizzying *escaramuza* (very intricate drill team patterns). All *charra* events are ridden in long skirts and performed on side saddle.

Escaramuza is frequently translated into English as "skirmish," which is accurate to a point. However, the Spanish term has an understood equestrian essence which is often overlooked by English interpreters, and it means: a small fight between soldiers on horseback. The drills performed by the *escaramuzas charras*, are highly athletic and graceful, but clearly convey in their choreography an artful appearance of a cavalry battle. In fact, the intricate crisscrosses, twirls, and sudden maneuvers of the women's exercises, often ridden at blazing tempos, are especially risky. Collisions can happen with serious consequences. Yet, *escaramuzas* inevitably seem to complete their equestrian maneuvers with apparent ease—truly a testimony to their riding skill, dedicated practice, and fine horses.

"We're doing what normally men can't even do on our horses . . . and riding side saddle!" Quiñones exclaims, with a good natured laugh.

The required attire should perhaps be added to that list of additional difficulties women riders face. Two kinds of riding outfits are allowed for *escaramuzas*: the *traje*, a tailored suit with skirt of a dark color, and the *Adelita* costume, the most often worn which is named for a legendary figure reputed to have been a revolutionary fighter and companion of general Pancho Villa—Kathleen M. Sands, in her great book, *Charreria Mexicana* (University of Arizona Press, 1993), describes this typical *escaramuza* outfit as: "a long skirt, *rebozo* [women's shawl] crossed over her bodice, and calf length boots [which] became popular during the revolution." These are typically accented with a rainbow of colors, fancy matching sombreros, and hair ribbons.

The Mexican *charro* saddle was not adapted for sidesaddle until 1925, and was done by Filemón Lepe, a *charro*, for his sister, Guadalupe. The *escaramuza* performances, however, were not seen in *charreadas* until decades later, in 1953. The vibrant female drills were instigated by a group of *charros* lead by Luis Ortega Ramos after they attended an event in Houston, Texas. These *charros* saw a group of twenty women riding astride in colorful outfits, with as many cowboys, performing a "carousel." It so impressed Ortega that he arranged a similar demonstration in Mexico City with children as riders which he called "Equestrian Carousel." This morphed into only girls, then they were switched to sidesaddle, and they toured with Ortega's *charro* show in Mexico and overseas. The act caught on with such excitement and popularity that individual *charro* groups began forming similar riding teams for women. They were soon renamed, *escaramuzas*, to commemorate the *charro's* revolutionary counterpart, the female riders of the revolution.

Even though the recent addition of charras into longer standing *charro* traditions shows an invention of the tradition, it does not detract from the lively, dazzling, and purely Mexican flavor of the *escaramuzas'* equitation. *Escaramuza* competitions are an even more recent addition to *charreadas*, not being initiated until 1989. Competitions require that eight *escaramuzas* perform together, but for exhibition that number can swell to a dozen.

Competition, explains Quiñones, begins at the local level with many different *charro* associations fielding *escaramuza* teams. The main states for these activities in the United States are California and Texas, with strong interest also seen in Arizona, New Mexico, Nevada, Kansas, Idaho, Colorado, and the city of Chicago, Illinois, she says. Then teams that win go on to compete at the pre-state, state, regional, and national levels. Those who win at the national level in the U. S. then gain the prestige of qualifying to compete in the Mexican national finals, held annually.

"It gives you a different level of the way people look at you," Quiñones says. "For a lot of us, it is that main goal of competing in Mexico, being proud that we're actually maintaining the tradition, and we're identified as a different equestrian group. This is my last year coordinating, but what I have found is that we're all basically working moms or daughters that are going to school. We're keeping our families together, including our horses—because that alone is dedication and care for them also. It's an uplifting spiritual thing.

"We're very jealous when our husbands try to take them [our horses] away! Sometimes they try to pull a quick one, 'Oh, I just need him for competition.' 'No, no, no . . . this is an *escaramuza* horse!'"

Men, however, also possess profound appreciation and respect for the *charras*.

"I can't imagine *charreria* without the grace, beauty, and source of pride the *escaramuza* brings to our traditional celebrations of culture, family unity, and competition," says Toby de la Torre, President of the Charros Federation, USA, and southern California representative for *Federacion Mexicana de Charreria*. "The *escaramuza* is a central link in the family chain of *charreria*. When I see a *charreada*, there are many things that make me swell up with pride and joy. I look in the stands and I see adoring family, friends, and fans . . . Grandmas and Grandpas, Auntees and Uncles, cousins and friends, sons and daughters. They are there to see their loved ones practice the beloved traditions. I can't separate the memory of the pictures of the *Adelitas* (as *escaramuzas* are respectfully referred to as) side by side with the men in battles of the revolution era. Now they are by our side again, continuing the fight for pride, tradition, and family unity. The *escaramuzas* also have that extra woman's caring touch and appreciation for their horses and attire that helps keep us in check— whether we like to admit it or not.

"*Que viva La Mujer A Caballo*!" he exclaims . . . . "Long live the horsewoman!"

CHAPTER 18

James DeBord and Joe. *(Mary Rudloff, Sample Media, Inc.)*

PBR PICK UP HORSE, JOE, RETIRED

James DeBord has been the subject of several articles I've written over the years. This one appeared in the January/February 2011 issue of Eclectic-Horseman magazine (www.eclectic-horseman.com). DeBord also factored into my recent book, Between the Reins (Spinning Sevens Press, 2010), when I recounted how he offered to haul two Quarter Horses, Jubal and Festus, from Dallas, Texas to Winston-Salem, North Carolina to help us provide them a home. Joe, his long time favorite bull pulling horse, won the hearts of many fans, and it was very gratifying that editor Emily Kitching at Eclectic-Horseman was happy to run this story on such a notable horse's retirement.

Last year at the Professional Bull Riders (PBR) World Finals in Las Vegas a long time PBR regular retired after a stellar career . . . but when this arena champion got put out to pasture, it's no joke, he really got put out to pasture. He's not a bull rider, or a bull, but Joe, a veteran PBR pick up horse. The familiar gray Quarter Horse gelding wrapped up his nine year career with the PBR at the completion of the 2009 season.

James DeBord, of Yoakum, Texas, Joe's owner and PBR Safety Rider (the title given pick up men in the PBR), explains, "He's 20 years old, and he's been doing it [bull roping and ranch work] for 17 years. I want to retire him while he still can do a good job. I don't want to just go out there and rope bulls on him until one day he just won't pull one out. He's been a good horse. He deserves better than that."

Joe spent the last nine years of his 17 year career as a working ranch and rodeo horse criss-crossing America with the PBR's televised Built Ford Tough Series events. The job won him many admirers among the top bull riders in the world that he helped to protect.

"I've seen that horse since James came around," says three time PBR World Champion, Adriano Moraes, "and Joe really impressed me because he's not the biggest horse, he's not a giant, but he pulls like one. That horse just has that much heart and desire and joy in what he does. You can see he is always calm. He's always alert. He knows what he's doing. You know it's safer when James is there, especially riding Joe. If there is a very bad case of a hang up where they'll have to stop the bull, James and Joe will step it up and they will help the bullfighters do their job. If the bull hits the fence—if for some reason it comes loose—we know that that bull will not go far because James and Joe will rope them and bring them back. Knowing that my sport is safe, not just for me but also for the spectators, is a very good feeling."

Many spectators learned Joe's name over the years and are real fans of the horse, says DeBord. The gray gelding made countless cameo appearances during televised events as well, often visible in quick camera shots of wrecks when a bull is roped, or simply moving in to help usher an obstinate bull out of the arena.

"I've seen a lot of people rope bulls on good horses, but I've never seen one better than [Joe]," says PBR Livestock Director and Vice President, Cody Lambert. "I've ridden him a couple of times and roped a few bulls—I don't think you could hook onto anything he couldn't pull. It's just amazing, really. He just leans into it, and however much it takes, that's how much he puts into it. Joe gets the job done every time—he's always been great—but James could get on a donkey and make him look good."

James DeBord and Joe at work roping a bull at a PBR event.
(Mary Rudloff, Sample Media, Inc.)

DeBord says for such an exceptional ranch horse, Joe's chance to prove himself nearly ended before it began. The cowboy was doing some day work at a nearby ranch for the Mussellman Cattle Company, and he noticed the young horse corralled with a bunch of older horses headed for the sale barn. Joe was considered by the crew too wild to train, with a track record that included above average bouts of bucking and striking out. $400 saved Joe from his demise, and DeBord trailered home his new project.

"One of the stock handlers told me one time," DeBord says, chuckling, "'That horse has made you famous.' I just kinda thought to myself, well maybe I made him famous 'cause when I got him he was an old outlaw. He's pretty exceptional to be able to do what he's done that long. To be able to rope that many bulls. I know one weekend I probably roped sixty bulls on him."

"Heart" is the word that gets used to describe Joe most. Two time PBR World Champion and the bull rider with the most 90+ careers rides, Chris Shivers, knows about heart and knows Joe personally.

"I've seen that horse a ton of times," says Shivers, "and [DeBord] always gets lots of big stuff roped on him and I've never seen him quit, not one time. I've never seen him bog him down where he couldn't pull a bull out of the arena with him. I've rode the horse some. I think James has rode that horse probably a million miles, you know, working cattle and other things, then he comes to the big show [PBR Built Ford Tough Series] . . . the horse is not that big, he weighs probably less than twelve-hundred pounds, but I've seen him drag two hundred bulls out of the arena—he's got a big heart for a little horse."

Joe is even better in the arena than he was a decade ago, according to DeBord. Retiring him last year was a decision made out of respect for the horse's accomplishments and age, but in no way a reflection of his performance, which remains top notch.

"I was going to retire him [the year before at Vegas]," DeBord confesses. "My hat had got pretty dirty . . . I was sitting in my trailer brushing it off with a horse brush, and it was kinda windy that day and the wind blew my hat out of my hand and it blew it over there by him—he was standing right in the door with me—I'd just got through saddling him, and he kicked at it just like he was trying to kill something! I said, 'well, if you can do that you can go one more year.'

"I'd rather use him than any one I got," DeBord says. "A lot of those horses, they get too scared of those bulls, and when a wreck's going on ol' Joe, he'll just let you ride right up in the middle and just stay there till you need to leave. Where some of those other ones, they're not wanting to get there to start with. They'll try to run off and get away from it."

Joe and DeBord traveled together to their final PBR Finals in 2009. Then, it was back home to Yoakum for Joe for good.

"I just turned him out." DeBord continues. "I've got some young ones coming up that need riding anyway. Every now and then . . . like the other day, I took him along . . . a guy needed a horse to ride to pen some cattle with, so I took him 'cause the guy didn't ride all that well and I knew he was dependable enough for him.

"A lot of people have tried to buy him—you just don't sell one like that."

CHAPTER 19

The seasonal nature of ranching in Texas creates the
additional need for cowboys at certain times of the year.
(Bob Moorhouse)

TEXAS DAY WORK COWBOYS

The May 2008 issue of America's Horse included this feature.

The American Quarter Horse is such a versatile breed that his job description in these modern times runs the spectrum of equestrian endeavors from performance cow horse sports, to racing, to dressage, to trail riding . . . but the Quarter Horse remains unquestionably the single dominant figure still hard at work in the demanding world that formed the breed in the first place—the ranch. Times change and so has the business of beef. In the present climate of Texas ranching, cowboys and Quarter Horses still have work. Some of these positions are full time, but typically ranches these days depend on day work cowboys to provide much of their labor needs. Often these day workers have their own string of Quarter Horses, so when a ranch hires the hand to work for a bit, it hires these tenacious and capable horses as well.

The nature of cattle ranching creates spikes in the need for labor. Branding time and weaning time, for instance, are yearly occasions when hiring extra hands on a ranch is helpful, if not downright essential. The day worker spends most of his working hours in the saddle. Hundreds of thousands of acres of terrain of all kinds are covered by cowboys to make ranching a viable business in Texas alone Some of that is so rough it is only accessible horseback, making capable riders and horses absolutely essential to the task. The jobs they perform range from rounding and moving sizable herds across wide spaces, to roping, cutting, and sorting cattle.

In the modern economy, day working on larger ranches still provides regular seasonal work for some cowboys every year. For many, day work on larger ranches can be supplemented with other hit-or-miss cowboy day work and various types of part-time work and can add up to a living. A few cowboys even make their living entirely off of day work. Regardless of whether the work schedule fits together smoothly over the year, or is a less dependable, if not hand-to-mouth prospect—for some folks the option of working from the saddle on their Quarter Horses for any part of their livelihood is the biggest paycheck of all.

Mike Seago

One cowboy who knows both sides of the day work equation is Mike Seago. Seago spent 16 years at the famed Four-Sixes Ranch, based in Guthrie, Texas. The last nine of those he held the position of wagon boss, which placed him just under the ranch manager in hierarchy, and in charge of all the cowboy help on the whole outfit, including hiring and firing both full time and day work cowboys. For over six years now he has been based from his own place in Paducah.

"A single guy can make a living at it," Seago says of day work cowboying, "but a married man . . . you've got to have something else. I have a few cows of my own. I've got 40, and I have a partnership with my son-in-law on 275 others. And I sell some liquid feed in the winter."

Seago says that during the time he worked at the Sixes some of the full time positions dwindled to where now nearly all the help but a skeleton crew is made up of day workers. This is a regular trend, he says, and is a result of it becoming increasingly difficult to make a profit ranching. The other side of that coin is that the demand for day workers is substantial. A dependable hand with a decent string of ranch horses can find himself very much a hot commodity in ranch country during the busy times these days.

"The bad thing about day working," Seago says, "is that you might be out of work for a month. Bad weather can knock out a day here or there, or a week even. It takes a lot of little deals to make things go."

Seago is married and has his own place with horses and cattle with the many responsibilities that come along with them. He is fortunate to live in an area that is close enough to several ranches, like the Triangle, the Matador, the Pitchfork, and the Four-Sixes, to allow him to go to work and return home each evening. His wife has a full time position working for the United States Department of Agriculture, which also helps even out the patchy flow of day work income.

"Most of the ranches in the area hire me for usually a week at least. When I start with a ranch, I'm gonna be there till they get

A dependable hand with a string of capable ranch horses
can stay in demand in ranch country. *(Bob Moorhouse)*

through. Most of them I trailer back and forth. I've got a trailer
with a living quarters in it, but 90% of it I just trailer out of here
because it's not far. Cows I can tend to on weekends, but the horses
I need to tend to daily. I raise a few horses—broke them all my life,
and I did it for the Sixes."

It's not hard to get Seago talking about his Quarter Horses,
like Taffy, a dun gelding who is a grandson of Doc Quixote out of a
Peppy San Badger mare.

"Of course, all mine are registered Quarter Horses," he
offers. "They're the only ones I ever rode. I've got five geldings
here that I day work off of. They're all gettin' pretty well seasoned,
dragging calves and cutting 'dries.' I feel like any of those five I
could put in a full day's work on, and it doesn't matter how hard or
easy [the work is]."

Aside from the string of working geldings, Seago also has a seven year old red dun stallion High Brow Senior that works on ranches occasionally and shows in ranch horse cutting competitions. He is called "Hic" because he's a son of High Brow Hickory. Seago has twice qualified on him for the finals in his area and plans to do a lot more showing on him this season.

Larry Abbot

When asked how long he's been cowboying, Larry Abbot replies, "How long? All my life, I've always done it."

Abbot is still doing it as a day work cowboy from his home in Dumont, Texas. When he was younger, he day worked quite a bit. Later he spent some years working full time as a spur and bit maker, and then he managed the Tongue River Ranch in Guthrie, Texas for 11 years. Only in the past five years has he returned to day working, which he, like Seago, must combine with other types of income to make a livelihood for himself and his wife.

"Most of them [the day workers] are the younger guys who can go to a ranch and stay three to four weeks, or even six weeks sometimes," Abbot explains—but he has responsibilities at home. "Right now I'm day working for the Pitchfork. That deal works for me because where I live is close to where the heifers are. I do it horseback. Prowl them horseback, on about 1800 acres."

A typical year for Abbot these days breaks down into a fairly regular seasonal routine. He starts in January taking care of the heifers that are calving at the Pitchfork until around the middle of February. Then there is a break in the cowboy work long enough for him to make a couple pairs of spurs and concentrate on his other side lines: truck trading and brokering a few cattle deals. Branding starts up in the first part of April, and the Pitchfork is where he mainly helps with branding. Abbot explains that one of the challenges to day working in that area is that all the ranches around tend to have a similar schedule. While a month may go by without any work, suddenly everyone is looking for experienced hands for the big jobs all at once, like branding for instance. It's a shame, he says, the scheduling couldn't be more staggered to allow for a hand to pick up brandings at two or three ranches, and thus turn several weeks of steady work into a month or two.

After branding is done, Abbot says he might catch a day or two on the smaller ranches in the region. The next chunk of regular work on a ranch comes in the summer at the McOwen ranch where the new calves are rounded up and their ears get tattooed.

Towards the end of summer he usually can pick up a little hit-and-miss work at the Triangle ranch. Around the first of October, his next serious job starts up again at the Pitchfork, which is weaning calves, a job that runs six weeks.

Abbot considers day working with his Quarter Horses pretty much an all around positive endeavor without much of a down side.

"I guess I like to work cattle, be horseback, and be around those type of guys," he says. "In this area, everybody knows everybody."

The only drawback to the business, he shares, is, "The price of gas!" A day worker, he explains, at most ranches can expect to be paid somewhere around $75 to $100 a day. By the time a cowboy spends $25 on gas—and that is if a ranch is fairly close to home—there is not much left over.

"If you blow a tire," he says, "going to work can actually cost you."

It is easy to get Abbot on the topic of horses, and if he's talking about horses, it is just a given he means Quarter Horses.

"I'm an older hefty guy," he exclaims with a laugh. "I like a shorter, stouter horse with a big barrel. They maneuver better than a horse that's kind of leggy. They have quick speed for catching cattle. You've got to have a horse with 'bottom' in 'em. You can go a long ways on him and still be able to get the job done when you get there."

In Abbot's line of work, he clearly requires a steadfast mount. His horses must be able to spend hours driving cattle over tough country, and then, once they're collected, still have the energy and ability to begin other tasks, like cutting and sorting them. When he sets out in the morning on one of his Quarter Horses, he says, that's usually the one he's on until quitting time.

Brother Daniels

Brother Daniels from Guthrie, Texas has relied on day working as a sole source of income for the past 10 years. Like Seago and Abbot, before choosing the route of a day worker, Daniels held steady ranch jobs for many years.

"I don't feel so tied down," Daniels says of day working. "I feel more freedom."

During the first five years of steady day work, Daniels says he worked at ranches within about a hundred miles from home. In the last five, though, he has widened that area and goes as far as Arizona and New Mexico.

"Most of these ranches you can count on for being busy for about five weeks through the 'works'—like branding and weaning," he says. He points out that the Four-Sixes and the Pitchfork ranches are both close to home for him, and adds, "I stay pretty busy just between those two ranches."

"Most of the places allow you and your horses to stay and feed you and your horses," Daniels explains. "If I was driving everywhere, I couldn't make that work. It's too expensive. You'd have to be a little bit more of a businessman than I am."

Unlike Seago and Abbot, Daniels is single and doesn't own land, which makes day work income, and the ability to be more nomadic, an easier prospect. His home base in Guthrie is owned by his mother. As for learning the trade of cowboying, he says he just grew up doing it.

"My daddy was a real good cowboy," he says. "He died when I was 15, but I was pretty much made by then. It's all I ever wanted to do. What I've always liked best is being horseback and being outdoors. I'm 47, and my horses are my kids. I have three right now. That's not really enough. You need four or five at least. Especially a day worker 'cause you're always horseback working. I'll get through at a ranch, and those guys [the regular ranch hands] can turn their horses out for a break, but I've got to go to the next place and go right back to work horseback."

Most of the outfits where he works have horses that he can ride when his need a break.

Rockin Peanut Jack, who Daniels calls Rocky, is a registered Quarter Horse in his string, and he believes Quarter Horses are the breed for the type of work he does.

"They're just cowey, for one thing," he says. "To me, they're built just right to handle themselves correct. Stop hard. It's just natural for them to do."

One essential aspect of getting repeat work as a day worker, according to Daniels, is in one's job ethic. Basically, a day worker is free to come and go, but being too fickle and leaving a ranch when it is time to get down to work can shoot a fellow in the foot and hurt his chances of getting hired onto that ranch again. Repeat seasonal work at the larger ranches is the one steady source of income a day worker in Texas can depend on. Losing those opportunities could easily ruin a day work cowboy's chances to stay working at all.

"A man has to be a good person and do the right thing," Daniels insists when talking about day working at ranches. "When I hire on a ranch, I stay till the work is through. I'm friends with all of them, so they'll help me out. It's very important to do the right thing . . . probably more important than being a good hand."

CHAPTER 20

Tom and Cate. *(Ken Moates)*

CATE THE BIG RED MULE

This essay was written around 2006, not long after the events it describes occurred. Equus magazine scooped it up immediately, but it ran only recently in the May 2011 issue as a "Back Page" essay. This is a slightly longer draft than the edited version that was published. Cate kept us company for a year and a half before passing away one evening simply from old age as far a anyone could tell. She is buried on our farm.

A small handwritten note taped to the feed store window caught my eye as I pushed the door open. I stopped half way in and backed out again to read it . . . then panicked!

The note said, "Pulling Mule for Sale" in the neat, legible cursive writing typical of the generation before mine. I didn't recognize the number, but I was certain who that mule must be . . . it had to be Cate.

This story starts a decade earlier. My wife Carol noticed the mule probably the first day she arrived in her pasture on a main road nearby. "Look at the beautiful big red mule!" she said every time we passed by . . . for the next two years.

Every trip that way became an opportunity check on the Big Red Mule. Where is she? What's she doing? Carol was so smitten that my standing joke has been, "If that Big Red Mule had been a Jack instead of a Jenny, she would have left me for it long ago."

After a couple of years of this obsessing, the longing to see the mule up close overpowered Carol and prompted us to stop in out-of-the-blue one day and ask to be formerly introduced to The Big Red Mule once and for all. The owners were Bud and Elizabeth (pronounced, 'Liz-Beth). Luckily, they were warm and inviting and happy to talk mule. And Carol got a glowing moment of epiphany getting to run her hands through the mule's thick red coat and tell the girl how special she was.

The owners were married just a few years before, both well into their fifties. Bud was a tall, powerful, sturdy man; he was from Kentucky where he'd worked with mules his whole life on farms and logging operations between stints of working in the coal mines. 'Liz-Beth was an interesting contrast, a short jolly energetic woman always laughing with a braid running down her back and wearing a pretty apron throughout the day (not just in the kitchen) in the traditional manner of this Appalachian region.

Cate, we learned, was the Big Red Mule's proper name. From the road, her beauty is obvious, especially the way the white muzzle and circles around the eyes along with the big floppy ears present the sweetest effect—but up close, one is first enamored by the sheer mass of her size. She's huge! Her dam was a Belgian, and she certainly carried her mother's traits, and the mammoth Jack sire must have been no slouch either.

Bud sold firewood and Cate pulled logs for this venture. She had other talents, as well. Before long Carol was back at their place photographing Cate all harnessed up pulling a plow, carefully placing each foot in the furrow as she went along, with Bud walking behind.

Eight years passed. Our constant monitoring of Cate's pasture endeavors (usually exciting observations like: "Oh look . . . she's laying down!" or, "Miss Cate's standing in the barn!") continued unabated. Then the note appeared on the feed store window. In an instant, the whole balance of the universe tipped. Cate was a constant in this world, always there—maybe out of sight behind the barn, but, like the sun behind a cloud, still always there.

Reading the note was at once a grave concern—Why are they selling her? Who might buy her? Would they take care of her?—and one of those personal moments, like losing someone close, when you are brought smack against the realization that life, with all of its many elements we love and come to depend on, doesn't last forever.

So I rushed into the store. "Is that Bud and 'Liz-Beth's mule for sale?" I asked frantically. But I knew the answer already.

I went back to the car where Carol waited and told her. We drove straight there. Bud was gone, but 'Liz-Beth filled us in; Bud had been fighting lung cancer, and while he was doing well now after surgery, he could no longer work Cate. They needed to sell her.

It wasn't on the agenda to get another equine to go with the other three here, nor was it in the financial plan (especially just before the Holidays as it was), but there was little debate. She came to her new home to the relief of all involved. Now, Cate warms us every time we go in or out of our place and check out what she's up to in her pasture. Cate stays with Carol's other big red equine heart throb, her sorrel gelding Niji, so she can go anytime and soak up all the radiance she can stand from these two.

This may be a new home for Cate, but it's one, oddly enough, she already has been a part of for a decade, in our hearts and minds.

ABOUT THE AUTHOR

(Harry Whitney)

Tom Moates is a leading equestrian journalist and author. This award winning writer is on the masthead of *Equus* magazine as a Contributing Writer, where his work frequently appears. Articles he pens run in many major horse magazines in the United States and abroad including *The American Quarter Horse Journal, Eclectic-Horseman, The Trail Rider, America's Horse, American Cowboy, Paint Horse*

Journal, Western Horseman, and *Hoofbeats* (Australia). *Discovering Natural Horsemanship, A Horse's Thought,* and *Between the Reins,* his first three horse books, are firmly established titles in the library of modern equestrian literature. Moates lives on a solar powered farm with his wife Carol and a herd of horses in the Blue Ridge Mountains of Virginia. Book ordering info and Moates's latest publishing news are available at www.TomMoates.com.

www.ingramcontent.com/pod-product-compliance
Lightning Source LLC
Chambersburg PA
CBHW020245290326
41930CB00038B/393